Deference to the Marketplace:

A Case Study of the Role of the Ontario Municipal Board
in Agricultural Land Conservation, 1975-1985

David McRobert

Fellow, Faculty of Environmental Studies

Student, Osgoode Hall Law School

York University, Toronto, Ontario

May 1986

Table of Contents

The loss of farmland is of very real concern for us, even though it is hard to quantify. I use the analogy of a bologna you have in your refrigerator at home. Everybody comes along and takes a small slice. You don't notice because what's another little slice. And then one day you look around -- and it's just about gone.

                    Stephen Wilgar(1)
                       Chairman
          Grocery Products Manufacturers
                      of Canada

Introduction

The disappearance of Canada's agricultural heartland is a process that has been underway for several decades. As cities like Toronto, St. Catherines, Winnipeg, Calgary and Regina expand, they gobble up much of the best farmland in the nation. Although the process parallels that ocurring elsewhere in the industrial world, Canada has one of the worst records over the past two decades on this conservation problem.(2)

Most of the land that is appropriated for industrial, recreational and residential uses never reverts back to agriculture. Thus, some observers charge that this process of urbanization could destroy Canada's most productive agricultural lands over the course of the next generation if it is not controlled in the future.(3)

In this paper some of the legal aspects of regulation for agricultural land conservation (ALC) in Ontario over the past decade are explored. One of the goals will be to review some of the decisions on ALC made by the Ontario Municipal Board (OMB), the governmental tribunal responsible for regulating land use planning. In addition, an attempt will be made to illuminate the weaknesses in the current planning and regulatory procedures as illustrated by these decisions and to identify some potential improvements that might be made.

The structure of this paper reflects the complexity of the problem of ALC. To do the subject justice, this paper ranges over a wide ambit of materials and examines numerous issues. These include the historical background to the problem, a general introduction to land use planning in Ontario, the role of the OMB, and the structural barriers to implementation of long-term solutions to ALC within a "free market" paradigm. In addition, the evolution of the specific policies on ALC promoted by the province of Ontario will be summarized. First, though, the problem must be more fully described.

Grappling with ALC: The Facts.

In the late 1960s and throughout the 1970s a flurry of legislation was enacted to promote ALC in North American jurisdictions. Since then, the debate over whether these initiatives were successful and can even be justified has persisted in most of these areas. There have been calls for a national policy to address the problem in the United States. (4) Moreover, questions have been raised about whether land should be treated as a commodity at all because of its importance to the long-term survival of humanity and problems in the rest of the world with food shortages. (5)

Despite these arguments, farmland conservation is by no means a straightforward issue. Developers, farmers and municipal councillors in rural areas and the rural/urban fringe in southern Ontario have begun to make their voice heard as well and what they are saying challenges the idea that most people tacitly endorse ALC. In essence, these opponents of ALC resent agricultural land preservationists who continue to fight mainly local battles and generate support for their agenda. Amid claims there is no shortage of developable agricultural land in Canada, ALC advocates find growing resistance to their repeated efforts to amend laws and strengthen existing programs.

The range of views on the problem suggest at least two different paradigms exist on the need for ALC. The first paradigm, promoted by the conservationists, holds that all agricultural land should be protected whenever possible. The second, which the latter group of developers and municipal politicians uphold, supports the idea that other competing interests also have to be weighed.

The more vocal minority perspective on ALC is presented by conservationists, who, over the past decade, have gained access to various fora to present their views. For example, the recent Royal Commission on the Economic Union and Development Prospects for Canada (the Macdonald Commission) heard testimony from many conservationists on the problem of ALC and apparently their submissions were put forward to a fairly receptive audience. Thus, the Agricultural Institute of Canada warned that the nation faces potentially serious problems in maintaining its supply of productive agricultural land in the next few decades:

> Even in the recent past Canada's legislators and the Canadian public believed that Canada has almost inexhaustible supplies of land for farming. Also, they were convinced that improved agricultural technology and its application would ensure the availability of

farmland forever.

These misconceptions have created a misleading impression of abundance and have resulted in land use practices which are precipitating some major concerns....(6)

The problem of perception which the Institute identifies is no doubt at the root of the skepticism that some people have about the need for ALC. Not surprisingly, the implicit ambivalence which stems from misleading perceptions of the problem partly explains why the the issue has failed to generate a broad base of political support. However, it is also clear that there has been a failure on the part of advocates on both sides to fully explain the ideas and philosophy that underly their paradigm about ALC.

This ambivalence is highlighted in the debate about ALC in Canada at present. There are, it seems, as many questions about the issue are there are clear answers. The Macdonald Commissioners reflect call for a comprehensive study of the loss of this valuable land to urban sprawl:

> How rapidly is this loss proceeding? Does it represent a failure of the private land market? That is, are we ignoring important social considerations in tolerating a situation in which urban developers can consistently outbid farmers for agricultural land? Is a development freeze -- a solution that has been tried in some jurisdictions -- an adequate solution, or are there better avenues to try? (7)

Some of the issues raised by the Commissioners in this passage will be considered in the analysis below. As the quotation suggests, part of the difficulty with generating political support for ALC is that perceptions differ as to whether concerns over disappearing farmland are justified and how the state can intervene to protect its interests without seriously curtailing the right of private individuals to develop land.

Admittedly, the case for ALC is not clear-cut. Clearly, there is no shortage of food in Canada today even though nature's bounty is not always equally distributed. In fact, the recent problems of oversupply(7a) suggest that there is a need to discourage production. However, simplistic supply management will not solve all of the problems faced by farmers; changing diets and lifestyles are also responsible for the decline in demand for certain commodities such as tobacco, red meat and potatoes.

International forces must also be taken into account as they are relevent to the success of Canadian farmers and the perceived need for ALC. In the recent past, fruits and vegetables from Mexico, California, South America and Europe have become more readily available in Canada. Critics point out that it is dangerous to rely on a supply that may not be secure over the long term. In their view, it is a mistake to allow Canadian farmland to disappear because food prices on the international market in the short term are unrealistically low.

Defenders of existing approaches are unperturbed by these criticisms of current food policy in Canada. They point out that improvements in farm technology have already resulted in significant increases in food production in Ontario over the past three decades(8) and that these trends are likely to continue as a result of irradiation and biotechnology and other developments.

Statistics show that the average farmer in North America produces enough food to feed more than seventy people, which is more than four times the amount produced in the 1940s. It is possible that this rate of increase could continue. (8a)

A collateral argument that is now gaining popularity in the United States is that ALC is not a good thing because prime farm land is also prime building land and there is a housing shortage in most of urban North America. At the same time this argument holds there is no food shortage in either the United States or Canada. Thus, critics of ALC argue that there is nothing about agricultural land that makes it more suitable for agriculture than tarmac. (8a*) In their view the market should rule, and ALC should not be promoted at the expense of housing or other important urban projects.

Advocates for ALC tell a different story, contending that Canada needs all its land for the future. Moreover, some of the more radical exponents of the conservationists paradigm maintain that most of the food production advances in the last twenty years have taken place because increasing amounts of energy and fertilizers are being employed in agriculture. (8b) Recent reports show that these practices are having a devastating impact on soil quality and amount to "mining the soil." Thus, the conservationists claim that Canada is mortgaging its future by paving over some of the best farmland in the nation. Our current illusion of plenty will fade when the price of food increases substantially in the next century and the capacity to produce valuable fruits and vegetables has been irretrievably lost.

The most important of the facts supporting this critique of current food and ALC policies relate to the amount of land available for future production. In the 1960s and early 1970s, the federal and provincial governments prepared a detailed survey of Canada's land resource,(9) which revealed that only 11 per cent of Canada's land is capable of sustaining agricultural production. In addition, the study also determined that only 5 per cent of this land can produce crops and a mere 0.5 per cent is valuable class-one land which is capable of sustaining higher quality fruit and vegetable production.(10) Thus, while Canada is the second-largest country on the planet, our stock of land available for agricultural production is roughly equivalent to the area of Sweden and our prime agricultural land base is smaller in area than New Brunswick.(11)

To many Canadians this area may still seem enormous, especially in comparison to the amount of land available in many densely populated countries such as Japan and China. However, according to critics, there is no reason to be complacent about ALC in Canada. Most of the best agricultural land in many provinces is located near our largest cities, which are expanding at a remarkable pace; if current patterns continue, a large amount of this class-one land could be lost by the end of the century. These trends also cast doubt on whether the prospect of a sustainable food supply can be sustained in Canada into the next century. As the maps in Figure 1 show, an enormous amount of land has been lost already.

Admittedly, these trends are more a reflection of the historical development of the nation, rather than any deliberate plot to urbanize prime agricultural land. Most of the towns that grew into major cities were situated on the banks of major rivers in fertile valleys, where settlements were bound to grow. Up until the 1960s and 1970s it did not appear that this pattern should be a concern; most Canadians believed that there was plenty of land available which could be drained and converted to agricultural use. Recent studies have shown that poorer quality land is very expensive to develop however, and the ecological consequences of land drainage are often severe. (11a)

As a result, some forward-thinking geographers and environmental scientists began to question whether the growth trends around these urban centres apparent in the 1960s and 1970s could be justified over the long term. Studies undertaken subsequently have shown the amount of farmland in Canada which was converted to direct urban use between 1966 to 1976 was equivalent to an area the size of the city of Hamilton. Moreover, of the land converted, 63 per cent was rated in the top three classes for agriculture. (12)

Ontario has probably been the worst offender over the past few decades. A considerable proportion of Canada's prime agricultural land is located in southern Ontario. As the Macdonald Commission recently observed, "37 per cent of Canada's class-one agricultural land and 25 per cent of our class-two land can be seen from the top of Toronto's CN tower." (13) Since this area is also one of the most rapidly urbanizing parts of Canada, it is not surprising that much of the rural land converted to urban uses in southern Ontario is class-one farm land.

The Macdonald Commission warns against complicity on the problem of ALC, especially among residents of southern Ontario, because of the quality of land being sacrificed:

> In considering this loss, we must be chary in taking comfort from the increases in total hectarage that come from improving land. There is no benefit in replacing land that can grow fruits, vegetables and corn with land suitable only for barley or hay. (14)

The Commissioners also point out that some of the crops grown in certain areas such as the Golden Horseshoe, "cannot be produced commercially in any other part of Canada."(15) This conclusion would seem to support the contention that Ontario has a special responsibility to protect this prime farmland for the use of future generations, if only to guarantee security of supply of these food products in the next century for the rest of Canada.

The process of land appropriation is a much more difficult one to characterize, once the rationale for conservation has been articulated. Residents of major metropolitan centres have undoubtedly seen the process in action over the years, particularly if they venture out into the rural fringe of North America's major cities on a regular basis. The process is graphically illustrated in the Toronto area, where over two decades, the hinterland has receded into a practically continuous stretch of urban-industrialism, broken only by the pockets of greenspace in ravines or preserved for agricultural use.

Recent reports have shown that it is misleading to assume that this process of urban invasion on the outskirts of major centres such as Toronto Hamilton, and London, is responsible for most of the loss of prime farmland in Ontario though. (16) Although this invasive activity is often the most visible evidence of encroachment and seems most startling around large cities, small settlements with their rather generous space standards are causing a considerable proportion of urbanization on prime agricultural land. As the discussion below will suggest, one of the reasons why excessive amounts of farmlands are being zoned for urban uses is that many municipalities face serious financial difficulties presently and wish to raise badly-needed revenues by attracting new development. Thus, analysis of the issue of farmland conservation spills over into issues such as municipal financing and jurisdictional control.

Another factor contributing to the erosion of Canada's stock of farmland is the response of the farmers to the pressures for their land. Urban development is often percieved as inevitable and by the time developers make offers to purchase most land owners have more or less given up their attempts to continue farming. In part, this attitude reflects the experience of farming in the shadow of the metropolis; urban expansion creates problems for farmers because the new residents want to benefit from the more relaxed pace of their new environment and the amenities associated with rural living, but are often unwilling to pay some of the attendant costs including traffic delays on rural roads behind tractors as bales of hay are transported, and the health hazards of chemical spraying. The impatience of this new class of escapees from urban existence is demonstrated in their recent attempts to launch nuisance actions against farmers to curtail some of these practices. (16a)

Urban expansion creates other problems as well. The recent Senate Committee report, Soil at Risk, (17) noted that the heavily populated regions of Canada are subject to increasing pressure for building materials which are removed from agricultural lands. This creates problems because

> The removal of sand, gravel and stone for use in construction projects has disrupted the soil structure in some parts of this region. Some 165,500 acres (67,000 hectares) have been ruined for aggregates and, at least in the Kingston to Oshawa, 50% of this development is on Class 1 and 2 soils. This represents a loss of good soil since it is very unlikely that this soil can be reclaimed after the mining activity is over.

The report also notes that soil contamination is a growing concern, especially from sewage sludge, laden with heavy metals such as mercury, cadmium, arsenic and lead, and spread on farmland for fertilizer(18). Soil productivity and sustainability are also threatened by airborne industrial wastes.(19)

The growth of leisure and recreational activities on rural land is another contributant to the disappearance of productive farmland. The explosion of demand for campgrounds, cottage sites, highway picnic sites, parklands, race tracks, ski trails and other facilities has already taken its toll in southern

Ontario. (20) In addition, urban-related waste disposal problems are often exported to the hinterland, and these problems are imposing further demands on lands for "car graveyards," industrial wastes and land fill sites.

In concluding this introductory section, it is essential to bear in mind that all of the activities which now threaten the viability of sustainable production on Canada's agricultural land base have historically contributed enormously to the wealth of Ontario. Moreover, the provision of land for housing and industrial activities is important to the continued prosperity of Ontario. The challenge is to balance the disparate goals of conservation and development in order to reach a more appropriate long-term, sustainable approach to ALC. In this paper, the attempt by the OMB to find this elusive balance will be examined. However, first the evolution of government policies on ALC in the modern period must be traced to show why measures intended to halt the current patterns of development on farmland in southern Ontario have so far largely failed.

Historical Sources of Government Policies

To set this analysis in context, it is important to consider some of the political, legal and technological factors which have shaped ALC policies in Ontario over the past four decades. As will be argued below, the continued failure to devise policies and programmes to conserve land for agricultural purposes suggests that there are deeply-rooted, historical and economic forces at work thwarting ALC.

Agriculture has always played an important role in Ontario's economic development and up until the early 1940s, was dominant. However, as Rhea notes in his survey of Ontario's economic history between 1939 and 1975, manufacturing, the service sector and other activities ousted agriculture of its prominence.(21) It is important to review briefly the implications of this trend because it implies certain policies towards renewable resources in general, and agriculture in particular, that foretold the fate of Ontario's prime farmland in the past two decades.

In theory, the renewable resource policies of the Ontario government during post-World War Two boom reflected a stated desire to balance the conflict between the perceived desire to promote economic growth and the recognition of a need to "conserve" forestry and water resources. However, in practice it is apparent that economic growth was emphasized more than conservation, as Rhea observes in the following passage:

> Whenever the provincial government could promote the utilization of a resource or expand the resource base by encouraging exploration and development, it continued to do so as it had in the past. Although it was also the government's declared intention to 'preserve and protect' renewable resources and the natural environment in general, it is difficult to find instances of conservation's being placed ahead of tangible and immediate economic benefits. (22)

Rhea goes on to observe that the main response to the pressure for conservation during this period was the creation of a Royal Commission on Forestry in the 1940s and the establishment of a Conservation Branch within the new Department of Planning and Development.(23) Moreover, the Progressive Conservative government's action in vesting a corporation with the right to pollute the Spanish River following the rancour which resulted from the famous KVP case(24) is probably an accurate guage of dominant political attitudes as to where the balance between conservation and development should lie.

The changes that took place in the area of ALC policy were less a reflection of deliberate policy and more a consequence of inadvertence. The amount of land classed as occupied farmland in 1941 was reduced from 10% to 7% by 1971. (25) Rhea notes that between the early 1940s and the 1970s the amount of occupied farm land fell at a rate of more than 17,000 acres per year. This shift partially reflects the declining importance of agriculture and the fact that decreasing inputs of labour and land were required to produce almost double the physical volume of agricultural production between 1939 and 1975 (see Table 1). These factors combined to encourage a mass exodus from farms in Ontario and an approximately 47 percent decrease in the number of farms during this period. (26)

Major changes in the amount of land used for food production and a gradual erosion of agricultural land supplies accompanied this exodus. Rhea describes the sources of the changes which eroded Ontario's food production base as follows:

> The reduction in farmland in Ontario during this period was the result of a number of forces that were working to reduce its value in agriculture relative to other uses. In the south-central part of the province there was a growing need for land to be used for urban residential subdivisions, for new industrial plants, for highway use, and as a source of gravel and other

building materials. Such requirements were
particularly intense near major centres of population,
especially in the countries adjacent to metropolitan
Toronto. In Halton country almost 42 per cent of the
1941 farm acreage had disappeared by 1971; in Peel the
loss was 40 per cent, and in York, 36 per cent. (27)

Rhea's characterization of the problem of ALC effectively
captures the dramatic changes over this thirty year. It remains
to document the impact of these changes on these regions over the
long-term and the kinds of alternatives that might have been
promoted if a different planning process had been in place at the
time.

That an alternative planning process which emphasized ALC
did not exist is probably a reflection of government priorities
at the time. Arguably, this pattern of urban encroachment on
prime farmland was largely implemented with the blessing of the
provincial governments, which, as Rhea observes, sought to
promote the expansion of housing and manufacturing activities
after the Second World War. This was a boom period for the
Canadian economy, and Ontario wanted to ensure that it gained a
large proportion of the benefits, even if development required
the sacrifice of agricultural lands to urban development
pressure.

The role of government in this urban development process was
mainly restricted to the promotion of home ownership and the
facilitation of municipal planning activities. Planners were
supposed to ensure not only that proper physical considerations
and site constraints were taken into account but also that social
services such as health and education were efficiently delivered.

Even when the need for a synthetic approach to planning was finally recognized through the initiation of the Design for Development Program(28) in 1970, the result was less than satisfactory:

> Despite repeated use of the word 'planning' and the elaborate studies generated as part of the process, the activity involved appears to have been little more than the co-ordination of various promotional programs. This function was not unimportant, given the increasing complexity of such undertakings caused by the proliferation of environmental protection regulations, land use restrictions, and local 'planning' activities. There was an obvious need for such co-ordination. Yet the setting of specific development goals and scheduling of measures to attain them seemed to get lost somewhere between the political and the merely administrative parts of the system. (29)

In this assessment of the provincial government's role in the promotion of economic growth, the nub of the problem of ALC in southern Ontario may be identified.

The dominant paradigm respecting residential density is another historical legacy which has a bearing on ALC. Its origins may be traced to the concerns of social reformers in Britain and the United States about the suffocating conditions that the early Industrial Revolution had produced in cities like London and New York. (30) By the turn of the century the seeds of current urbanization patterns had been sown in the minds of these reformers. For example, Ebenezer Howard(31) wrote in 1902 in his famous book Garden Cities of Tomorrow that England's urban blight could be remedied by building new towns in the countryside and protecting them from cities and one another by preserving the greenspace surrounding them.

These activists continued to lobby for the expansion of suburbs, an option that became more popular with the growth of automobile as a means of transport. Throughout the 1930s, influential planners such as Frank Lloyd Wright and Lewis Mumford advocated low-density development.(32) Wright's model city, Broadacre, called for a maximum of one family per acre, while Mumford held that no fixed density level was appropriate for all situations, the appropriate level being dependent upon the specific "social relationships to be served."(33) Although Mumford's approach was more advanced conceptually and recognized that commercial interests often were responsible for perceptions of urban congestion, it did not solve the problem of residential density regulation.

The eventual standards on residential density that fueled our current rapid urban encroachment on agricultural lands in southern Ontario were formulated in the early 1950s. Following the lead of their American counterparts, Canadian planners devised them to ensure that sanitation and safety from physical hazards, comfort, convenience and aesthetic satisfaction were emphasized in planning designs.(34)

Today, these standards continue to influence preferences and determine the nature of the housing market in most of North America.(35) Although condominium and apartment dwelling have become more popular in recent years, most people view home ownership as an important investment and goal in life. In addition, contemporary planning practice and conventional wisdom support the view that the marketplace should be the determinative force in guiding housing policies.(36)

This view seems untenable when the arguments made above about the need for ALC are considered. Low residential density housing and ALC seem almost mutually exclusive as long as population growth in southern Ontario continues unabated. Moreover, the continued significance of the planning standards that were formulated in the 1950s and 1960s is questionable. As the analysis above suggests, arguments for high residential density seem to be gaining increasing legitimacy. Many social scientists and planners are now advocating increased residential density, and their advocacy is supported by sociological and planning research.(37) There are also suggestions that it may be more economical to increase residential density because services can be provided more cheaply. Thus, changing attitudes towards residential and household density are the result of other forces in addition to ALC.(38)

To summarize, the problem of balancing development and conservation in Ontario is deeply rooted in certain historical patterns. These must be taken into account in analysis of the potential for ALC in Ontario. Moreover, these patterns have played a critical role in shaping the nature of land planning in Ontario today and the relative importance of ALC in the process.

Page 19

Land Planning in Ontario: A Short History

In Ontario, the main statute which governed land planning in both urban and rural areas for most of the period under consideration was the Planning Act. (39) This legislation has now been superceded but it is essential to compare and contrast both pieces of legislation to draw out the implications of the new Act for ALC in Ontario. Other legislation affecting land planning in this period included the Municipal Act, (40) the Planning and Development Act, (41) the Parkway Belt Planning and Development Act (42) and the Niagara Escarpment Planning and Development Act. (43) This legislative framework for planning and development control in rural areas is summarized in Table 2.

Many problems were identified in applying this institutional and legal framework. There were, it was argued, significant gaps and overlaps in the planning process, and certain issues, such as environmental protection, were often overlooked. (43a) In 1975, the Ontario government established the Planning Act Review Committee (PARC) under the Chairmanship of Professor Eli Comay to investigate, analyze and make recommendations for changes to this legislative framework. (44) Two years later, the report of PARC (often referred to as "The Comay Report") was released. The report suggested that planning practices in Ontario needed radical reform.

The Comay Report included several recommendations related to ALC; their thrust is reflected in the following passage from the subsection on environmental considerations in the chapter on municipal plans:

> 6.25
> Most municipal plans of recent years deal with environmental issues of some kind, with the coverage usually limited to matters concerning natural hazards, pollution and esthetics. The range of environmental concerns is broader in the currently emerging regional plans, a number of which place considerable emphasis on policies for the protection and management of major aspects of the natural environment. We have received numerous submissions that it be made mandatory that municipalities deal with environmental matters in their plans. (45)

Presumably this recommendation was intended to emphasize that issues such as ALC must be addressed by municipalities. (46)

The Comay Report was perceived as fairly innovative by some planners and academics, but was regarded critically by many other people. (47) The Ontario government responded with a White Paper in 1979 which toned down many of the Report's recommendations (48) and later that year they published a draft Planning Act based on their White Paper, for which they solicited comments on the proposed legislation. (49)

It was not until October 1981 that the proposed legislation received first reading; after the second reading, in February 1982, Bill 159 went to Standing Committee hearings. Over 360 briefs were received at these hearings. Many municipalities expressed anxiety about Bill 159 because they were uncertain about whether they could take over responsibilities that seemed implied in certain provisions of the new legislation, including its requirement that municipalities evaluate the impacts of major development projects, an exercize which undoubtedly would require additional staff. In an era of financial constraint, such provisions were regarded as extravagant by many rural municipalities with small budgets and constrained tax bases.

The revised Planning Act received third reading on January 25, 1983, and was proclaimed in force in August 1983. The legislation provides new administrative procedures by which municipal and regional governments can plan their land use, identify development objectives for their communities, prepare official plans, implement zoning by-laws, administer subdivision controls and severance consents, and regulate various activities within the confines of their jurisdictions.(50)

In the context of this study, the most important aspect of the Planning Act, 1983 is the approval procedure for official plans which are prepared by municipal councils and are subject to the approval of the Minister of Municipal Affairs. Any subsequent modifications to the official plan must also be referred to the Minister. The process may be illustrated as shown in Fig. 2.

The most important section of the new statute related to the approval process for official plans that are forwarded to the Minister is section 2 which requires the following:

PROVINCIAL ADMINISTRATION

2. The Minister, in carrying out his responsibilities under this Act, will have regard to, among others, matters of

provincial interest such as,

(a) the protection of the natural environment, including the agricultural resource base of the Province, and the management of natural resources;

(b) the protection of features of significant natural, architectural, historical or archaeological interest;

(c) the supply, efficient use and conservation of energy;

(d) the provision of major communication, servicing and transportation facilities;

(e) the equitable distribution of educational, health and other social facilities;

(f) the co-ordination of planning activities of municipalities and other public bodies;

(g) the resolution of planning conflicts involving municipalities and other public bodies;

(h) the health and safety of the population; and

(i) the protection of the financial and economic well-being of the Province and its municipalities.

Reconciling these different interests is easier in theory than it is in practice. All these different interests reflect competing goals which are not easily compromised in a democratic society where a landowner's freedom to develop land is highly valued. Land use planning seeks to limit this freedom "in the public interest" through regulation of siting and the imposition of zoning to minimize damage to land from industrial or commercial projects and protect the interests of landowners. (51) The basic idea behind this process is that a municipality should be able to prevent a private land owner from developing land in a way that is contrary to public policy. This type of regulation has been upheld as a valid limitation on civil and property rights almost

uniformly in common law jurisdictions for many decades. (52)
Intervention in land markets seems to be an important instrument
of public policy which has the broad support of the government,
the courts and the public(53?). As Stuart Proudfoot(54) has
observed:

> The rationale for governmental involvement in land
> markets on equity grounds has two dimensions:
> procedural and allocative. Procedural equity focuses
> on notions such as due process and equality of
> opportunity. Efforts to encourage greater citizen
> participation in the making of land use decisions is an
> example of an attempt to achieve procedural equity.
> Allocative equity has as its concern the outcome of
> decisions, i.e., who benefits and who loses from
> particular kinds of decisions. The two concepts of
> equity are related. For example, it may be argued that
> greater equity has been achieved through procedural
> changes for citizen input in land use decision making;
> we are thinking here of such devices as notice, public
> meetings, appeal provisions, and the like. The outcome
> of such participation in the form of substantive
> policies, however, may create inequities for groups in
> the community unable, for whatever reasons to
> participate in the process effectively.

Thus, Proudfoot maintains that the procedural and allocative
roles of land use planning foster greater equity in the economy.
This regulation of development compliments other forms of
controls and reinforces the liberal pluralist notion that the
state merely acts to balance competing interests in its
allocative and adjudicative function rather than to promote some
at the expense of others. (54a)

It is noteworthy this type of state regulation has come
under a significant and profound attack in recent years. (55) This
trend could influence the extent to which members of
administrative tribunals would be willing to intervene through

planning decisions in such a way as to "upset the market." The implications of this trend are unclear and the arguments in favour of a general movement towards deregulation in land planning seem dubious. Experience with issues such as environmental protection and ALC over the past decade does not support less regulation. Indeed, the Macdonald Commission supports increased intervention in the economy in these areas:

> In many other places in our Report, we call for less government intervention; in the area of environmental, however, we are obliged to call for more. Over the long term, the task of environmental regulation promises to be immense.... Consequently we recommend that governments increase their spending to provide the analysis needed to support the long-term regulatory task. (56)

A final issue to be considered is the likely impact of the Charter of Rights and Freedoms on land use planning in Ontario. There have been arguments that the Charter could expand public participation(56a), although strong arguments have been made in favour of limiting such rights as well. (57) The latter are usually predicated on the belief that intervenors merely exploit the public forums to promote their views as a recent decision of the European Court on Human Rights held. (58)

The Importance of the OMB

Administrative agencies play a number of roles in modern government. As the size and complexity of government has increased, the need for agencies to take over responsibilities that traditionally were thought to be accorded to ministers in

Parliament has also surged. The Ontario Municipal Board, established in 1907, is one of the most important administrative tribunals in the province,(61) although most people are unaware of its power wielded and the many roles that it performs in regulation of land use and financial arrangements in communities throughout Ontario.(62)

In this section, the role of the OMB as an administrative tribunal which guides and regulates municipal activities will be considered. The discussion will be split into four seperate subsections including: 1) the Roles of the OMB; 2) the Powers of the OMB as a decision-maker; 3) the OMB and the Environment; and 4) the OMB and government policy.

1) The Roles of the OMB(63)

Arguably, all administrative agencies perform a few roles for the state. Some of the roles of the Ontario Municipal Board (OMB) would include the following:

Assistant - In this role, the OMB takes some of the work load over from other branches of government and encourages a division of labour.

Substantive Expert - Given the complexity of government involvement in the economy as noted above, agencies like the OMB act as experts in substantive matters. Through hiring and retaining experts, the OMB can combine adjudicative and decision-making functions in a way that would be impossible or inappropriate for the courts or government.

Procedural Expert - The OMB has nurtured one of the most important new tools of government in Canada, the public hearing. Some of the structural advantages of employing agencies such as the OMB to examine problems include economy, speed in decision-making, ability to change quickly to meet changing conditions and freedom from legalistic procedures. In this sense, administrative agencies such as the OMB are nothing more than an alternate way of organizing and executing the functions of government. (64)

Adjudicator - Another role performed by the OMB is the adjudication of conflicts between private parties and the courts are not seen as a suitable form forum for their resolution. Since the OMB has relaxed rules of evidence and is not bound to rely on the interested parties to bring all the relevant evidence before them, it provides a middle ground between government departments and the courts. It is this quasi-judicial function which leads to the most frequent errors of the OMB. (65)

Rule Maker - Rule-making powers are often given to administrative agencies. These can include the power to fix procedures, criteria or policies in the regulation of highly complex or technical matters. The OMB has power to make rules governing its own procedures. In addition, a general non-statutory policy has been adopted by the OMB to follow its own past decisions, especially on cases with important social policy implications.

However, as we will see below, this rule-making could be subject to challenges in the future as a failure to exercise discretion.

Policy Maker - The power to make decisions on social policy manifests itself in the OMB's authority to approve official plan amendments, exercise discretion on referrals and interpret the mandate given to it by various statutes. This is the most controversial role which the OMB performs in a parliamentary system of government because it is often unclear where adjudication ends and policy-making begins. Consequently, it will be considered in much greater detail below.

Insulator - A final facet of the OMB's relationship to government is its purported independence. (66) As insulator between the public and government departments, agencies like the OMB make it much easier for the Ontario government to say "no" because it can honestly say the real decision-making power is outside its control, especially now that the appeal to cabinet route has been eliminated in the new Planning Act. (67)

Another role that the OMB performs in this respect is the insulation of municipal officials. In fact, it as been argued that municipal officials shifted their position on changes to the new legislation to maintain the OMB's authority for decisions and deflect responsibility if controversial land use conflicts arise. (68)

To conclude this survey of some of the functions of the OMB, it is essential to stress that there is a considerable degree of overlap among them, and that the new legislative provisions in the _Planning Act, 1983_ will cause some shifts in their relative significance. Although this is an arbitrary classification of the major roles performed by the OMB, it does serve as a useful framework for this discussion. In the balance of this paper, the record of the OMB on ALC will be considered in terms of this framework. The analysis will attempt to show is that the OMB has disseminated a model of non-regulation, or deference to the market, in land use planning decisions on ALC. This has been achieved through the strategic manipulation of the importance of their different roles of insulator, arbitrator and policy-maker to favour market economic processes in determining the nature and pace of urban development on agricultural land in southern Ontario.

2) The Powers of the OMB

The ability of the OMB to shape its mandate as a non-interventionist tribunal is partly attributable to the remarkable powers granted by the government in its enabling legislation. Cynics have claimed that the OMB has more power than the highest courts in the land because it is not bound by its own precedents and possesses the ability to uphold or deny the existence of an extraordinary range of rights. (69) Despite this, it is clear that Board decisions are reviewable by the courts and this acts to constrain their exercize of authority.

The exact powers of the OMB vary depending on the matter at issue. Under the former legislation, the OMB had power to approve zoning by-laws that did not conform with an official plan. In addition, the Board received referrals of sub-divisions and official plans and effectively exercized powers of approval that are exclusively held by the Minister. (69a) Although the Board's procedures are sometimes altered (this is usually done by the Board itself) the enabling legislation has not changed substantially since first enacted.

Municipalities and commentators on planning law in Ontario had for decades criticized the excessive powers wielded by the OMB and it came as no surprise that the Comay report recommended decreasing the role of the OMB in municipal planning. (70) The Committee did not see the current system as healthy in so far as the OMB had responsibility for making final decisions on planning matters. They recommended that the decision-making capacity should rest in the hands of the Minister and that the OMB should make recommendations to him based on the results of hearings. In addition, the Comay Report stated that the OMB should not determine provincial policy on planning matters and that it should review municipal decisions to ensure they are fair and reasonable. (71)

Another report released about the same time which was critical of the role of the OMB was the Report of the Royal Commission on Metropolitan Toronto. (72) This study also made recommendations which would have reduced the influence of the OMB.

What was the outcome of these recommendations? Not much, it seems in retrospect. The Planning Act, 1983 alters the position of the OMB, but most of the recommendations for structural change have been ignored. The prime role for the OMB under the new Act continues to be adjudication on references of proposed official plans. However, its role with respect to regulation of zoning by-laws has been narrowed; the Board now acts solely as an appellate tribunal on these matters. At the same time, the OMB still has a role to play on this last matter through its control over important financial decisions made by the municipality.

Consequently some planners argue that the ultimate effect of these minor changes has been to strengthen, rather than weaken, the position of the Board in municipal planning. With respect to the issue of ALC, it is apparent that the decision-making power of the OMB has not really altered. OMB decisions are still viewed as equivalent to precedent by most municipalities when they are considering an appeal of a ministerial decision on a planning matter. However, these municipalities are also aware that the Board is not bound by past decisions in their deliberations. This tends to present all sorts of opportunities for the OMB to vary its interpretation on discretionary complexities and play into the hands of municipalities who can support their argument for development through rational arguments defying conservation.

3) The OMB and the Environment

In considering the practices and procedures of the OMB in relation to ALC it is essential to consider, in a preliminary fashion, its approach to the natural environment in general terms. According to several decisions handed down in the 1970s, it is clear that environmental considerations are a valid planning matter. In the <u>Township of Westminister</u> v. <u>City of London</u>(73) Mr. Justice Houlden stated:

> ...it is most difficult to make a distinction between evidence which relates to environmental matters and evidence which relates to planning matters...the OMB should listen to the evidence presented to it without attempting to distinguish between environmental matters and planning matters.

Nevertheless, as Estrin and Swaigen(74) point out in their review of OMB decision-making on the environment, this does not guarantee that environmental considerations are given great weight. The Board's approach to onus of proof(75) has tended to ensure that challenges to official plans or plan amendments on environmental grounds are difficult to uphold. Moreover, individuals who have testified before the Board suggest that the composition of the panel is usually strongly determinative of the outcome. Estrin and Swaigen observe that the reactions of panel members to environmentalists and the issues they raised in the late 1960s and early 1970s ranged from indifference to rudeness and bullying.(76) While this observation may more accurately describe the attitudes of Board members in the early 1970s than it does today, there still are many individuals in the present group of appointees who downplay the role of conservation in planning decisions.

As a result the leading decisions of the Board on environmental issues do not suggest a clear-cut policy approach to balancing economic development and conservation objectives. While the OMB held for quite a long time that it was unreasonable for a municipality to engage in dollar-planning with respect to rezoning of neighbourhoods,(77) this precedent was set by Chairman J. A. Kennedy when popular concern for environmental issues had reached a peak of sorts in the late 1960s. Moreover, Kennedy demonstrated considerable sympathy to environmental concerns, recognized the need to preserve established stable neighborhoods and no doubt shaped board policy up until he resigned in 1971.

While the OMB still continues to give lip service to some of the principles articulated by Kennedy in the late 1960s, it is apparent that the body of precedent ha formulated for urban planning and zoning is not readily transferable to decisions on official plans and plan amendments. (78) The latter are much more broad decisions and the nature of the trade-offs to be made in these decisions is often blurred. As we will see below, the conflict is sometimes portrayed as one between those people who are for development and those who are against it. This kind of simplification seems to do little to help the cause of ALC and nature conservation advocates because it generates charges of elitism and creates a zero-sum game which is difficult to win. Moreover, this kind of adversarial situation is damaging in a recessionary period because the Board has reflected a much less sympathetic view on conservation and environmental issues in the recent past. (79)

This adversarial zero-sum game has especially high stakes in cases where municipalities are seeking official plan approvals. In an official plan hearing, the OMB's function is quite different from that performed in considering a zoning by-law. Since the implementation of official plans or plan amendments usually involves a departure from existing policy, the proposed changes require the OMB to take broader considerations into account. Nevertheless, the importance of related statutes and frameworks in promoting development suggest that the OMB's position with respect to ALC is constrained. (80) An understanding of the problem of balancing conservation and development requires

an examination of the interface between different statutes which
promote development planning and the private law doctrines about
property which seek to ensure that land is not wasted or used
inefficiently. Such a study would build on the notion that the
law illustrates a bias in favour of development; this bias is
rooted in what might be termed the "ecology of law"(81) rather
than any specific public policy or statutory device.

In the end, the success of any government measure in
overcoming this pro-development bias depends on the strength of
the new statutes enacted and policies developed by government.
This necessarily brings into sharper relief the issue of
interpretation of such measures by the Board and its view of its
obligation to apply government policy, assuming that sufficient
pressure can be brought to bear on the province to enact policies
that are sympathetic to the goals of ALC advocates. Thus, the
relationship between government policy and OMB practice is the
next matter which must be considered here.

4) The OMB and Government Policy.

Prior to the new Planning Act, the subject of government
policy statements was the subject of considerable confusion and
this resulted in extensive litigation on the issue. The main
source of confusion was that no central registry for such
statements and no specific legislation to authorize the adoption
of policy by the OMB existed. This situation led to the
implementation of Section 2 of the new legislation and the
formalization of government input to the OMB through Section 3.

The latter section of the Planning Act, 1983 will have a bearing on how policy is interpreted in the future by the OMB. It reads:

> 3. -- (1) The Minister, or the Minister together with any other minister of the crown, may from time to time issue policy statements that have been approved by the Lieutenant-Governor-in-Council on matters relating to municipal planning that in the opinion of the Minister are of provincial interest.
>
> (2) Before issuing a policy statement, the Minister shall confer with such municipal, provincial, federal or other officials and bodies or persons as the Minister considers have an interest in the proposed statement.
>
> (3) Where a policy statement is issued under subsection (1), the Minister shall cause it to be published in The Ontario Gazette and he shall give or cause to be given such further notice thereof, in such manner as he considers appropriate, to all members of the Assembly, to all municipalities and to such other agencies, organizations or persons as he considers have an interest in the statement.
>
> (4) Each municipality that receives notice of a policy statement under subsection (3) shall in turn give notice of the statement to each local board of the municipality that it considers has an interest in the statement.
>
> (5) In exercising any authority that affects any planning matter, the council of every municipality, every local board, every minister of the Crown and every ministry, board, commission or agency of the government, including the Municipal Board and Ontario Hydro, shall have regard to policy statements issued under subsection (1).

The critically important phrase in this new section is "shall have regard to". Undoubtedly interpretation of this phrase will be the battleground for future cases. As a guide to the kind of interpretation that the courts will uphold, it is essential to consider some of the leading decisions on the interpretation of policy by the OMB.

In terms of administrative law, the issue that interpretation of this phrase turns on is the jurisdiction of administrative tribunals and agencies. Numerous decisions have been rendered on this issue by the Ontario Court of Appeal and the Supreme Court of Canada.(82) Since it is not possible to review more a few of these decisions here, emphasis is placed on the decisions related to the OMB or cited in leading decisions on the OMB.

As a point of departure, it is noteworthy that the often quoted general statement of former Chief Justice McRuer in Re Jackson el al and Ontario Labour Relations Board(83) is usually accorded considerable weight in deliberations on role of tribunals and their jurisdictional capacities in Ontario. This statement holds that

> Under our form of Government the power of legislation is conferred on the duly-elected members of the Legislature ... (who decide) what jurisdiction will be conferred on an administrative tribunal.... It is no business of the Courts to consider whether it was wise or unwise to confer jurisdiction.... It is, however, the duty of a superior Court to be vigilant at all times to see that the jurisdiction conferred by the Legislature.... on an administrative tribunal, is adhered to by the tribunal, and that it does not enter upon an inquiry.....that it does not exceed its jurisdiction and that it does not deprive itself of jurisdiction to make a decision by doing an act that it is not authorized to do or by refusing to exercise the jurisdiction that has been conferred upon it by the legislative authority.(84)

In concluding that the Labour Relations Board was administrative, the Court held that it was within Board's power to accept the Minister's letter as part of the record of its hearings. This decision was applied in the Barrie Annexation case, and the result is that this approach to government policy has been formalized in Section 3 of the new legislation.

The obligation of the OMB to act fairly in considering the views offered by the public on policy matters is much less clear. Moreover, the weight that these considerations are accorded by the Board seems to be a largely discretionary matter. This has been confirmed by a long line of cases. In Re Cloverdale Shopping Centre Ltd. et al. v. Township of Etobicoke (85) the Court commented upon the kind of approach that the OMB should take to policy as follows:

> The Minister or the Board is not deciding a lis in the sense that the issue is confined to those for or against the proposal but he or it has to consider the safety, welfare and convenience, i.e., the interest of the public and the municipalities affected. In doing so the Minister or equally the Board is required to 'act judicially' but not beyond the sense that the parties are to be accorded a full and fair hearing and their submissions considered. When this has been accorded to the parties, the decision and administrative decision has then to be made. The decision is not a decision upon the objections to the proposal; those objections may be, and frequently are, of validity and importance; they may, however, be overruled upon the larger considerations of administrative policy.

Thus, when rendering a decision respecting an official plan the OMB maintains powers to formulate the policy it will employ. Presumably this applies to most administrative tribunals in Ontario and has a bearing on matters such as ALC and other environmental problems.

The result of this court decision if followed religously by tribunals such as the OMB would be that their decisions would become as predictable as the outcome of a lottery, according to some critics. One nevers knows exactly which government policy will be granted greatest weight and the tribunals are under no formal obligation to clarify what approach will be taken.

There are numerous disadvantages to this interpretation of how tribunals should interpret government policy. For example, it detracts from the goal of providing a stable and predictable climate for capital "investment". As a consequence, the OMB has tended to respond to pressures from the development industry and the courts by devising a consistent approach to government policy. The leading case on how the OMB interprets its role with respect to government policy is Re Township of Caledon Official Plan. (86) In this decision, former OMB Chairman Kennedy, stated as follows:

> ...under the Planning Act this Board is an administrative tribunal, often classed as a body exercising statutory powers. Since this Board therefore cannot be classed as a part of the judicial branch and since the Courts have held that this Board cannot legislate except as it may apply policy in a specific case and thereby create a right in some person, then this Board must form part of the executive branch of Government, an arm of the executive branch. On this reasoning it would be incongruous and perhaps contradictory if this Board were not obliged to follow Government policy.
>
> It must be made clear at once, however, the manner in which and the extent to which the Board is obliged to follow Government policy. To say that this Board follows Government policy is certainly not to say that it would or should seek to ascertain the wishes of the Government, the executive branch, in a particular case and then decide as the executive council may request,

or as any member of that council may request or
suggest. No, the Board does not and may not seek
advice or assistance from the executive council or any
member of that body in deciding an application before
it. The statutes provide that the Board must make the
decision and as stated above, the Board must hear
evidence, make findings of fact and apply policy to
those facts without any outside help.

Now the question remains, "What policy is to be applied
and how is it determined?" The Board applies its own
policy, of course developed as a type of jurisprudence
in its decisions over the years and constituting what
might be termed as a uniform approach. And there is
Government policy. This is found in the statutes, in
Government regulations which have statutory force, in
decisions of the executive council (the Cabinet) on
appeals from the Board, and in official pronouncements
by the Prime Minister or other Minister responsible in
respect of the particular subject-matter. It was
admitted by all counsel that Design for Development:
Toronto-Centered Region Plan is such an official
statement of policy.

This Board applies such a policy by considering and
interpreting the statement of policy with the
assistance of counsel after making findings of fact on
the evidence before it in much the same way as the
Courts apply the law by considering and interpreting
the pertinent law after making findings of fact on the
evidence before them.

The government states its policy as of general
application and this Board interprets and decides how
that policy applies to the facts in the particular case
without assistance from the Government or any member
and applies that policy for reasons which are given in
writing and which are subject to appeal to the Courts
on questions of law and to the executive council (the
Cabinet) on any question.(87)

As we will see below, this passage has been adopted by the
Supreme Court of Canada(88) as the key decision on the obligation
of the OMB to interpret Ontario government policy statements.
While it provides a somewhat clearer view of the OMB's
relationship to government, it does not resolve the ambiguities
surveyed above.

The leading decision on interpretation and application of government policy in Board decisions is the Barrie Annexation case. (89) The case arose in 1977 when the provincial government released a Task Force report on planning in Simcoe County. That report suggested that the City of Barrie would reach a population of 125,000 by 2011. In response the City devised a new official plan which annexed vast amounts of land in adjacent municipalities in order to provide the necessary space for such future growth and applied to the OMB to have their new boundary approved. (90)

The adjacent municipalities launched an apppeal against the annexation when the plan was submited to the OMB. They argued the population projections were unrealistic. The City of Barrie then asked the Minister of Treasury, Economics and Inter-governmental Affairs, Darcy McKeough, to direct a letter to the Board stating that the projections were based on government policy. The minister obliged. He released a statement which muddied waters by indicating it was government policy that communities such as Barrie were slated for growth according to Design for Development. (91)

When the hearings resumed, the Board ruled that they were bound by the policy statement in the letter and that there could be no cross-examination on the letter. Moreover, there could be no evidence led to contradict the population prediction of 125,000.

This ruling did not sit well with the Township of Innisfil. They sought to challenge the jurisdiction of the Board. (92) A court action was launched which is estimated to have cost more than $1 million by the time it was completed four years later. (93)

The first application went to Divisional Court of Ontario(94). It was dealt with by Robins J. there and the testimony for the trial interrupted the OMB hearings. The most contentious matter was the population projection. The opposing townships maintained this was totally unrealistic and said that a better figure would be approximately 75,000. They challenged the OMB's jurisdiction to follow the Minister's policy statement. In addition they challenged the fact that they were unable to cross-examine the Minister on this policy and the population estimates that had been made and that no evidence to contradict the population projections could be led.

On the first issue, Robins J. said the Board was not in law **bound** by this Policy Statement, but it had committed no jurisdictional error because <u>it thought</u> it was so bound:

> Once the Board concluded, as it did, that the preponderating effect of the policy statements was such that it was obliged to comply with it, that it so outweighed and overbalanced other considerations that it was to be followed, its conclusion is not reviewable by a Court. This is not a <u>jurisdictional issue</u> depriving the Board of the power vested in it; whether the Court may agree with ruling is not the issue; this cannot, in my opinion, amount to an error depriving it of the jurisdiction.

> It is said that the ruling under attack rendered the continuance of the hearing meaningless by so negating it that the Board could not satisfy its duty

to hold a hearing and deal with the application on the merits. I am satisfied that this is not so;....(95)

Robins went on to observe that

> ...by accepting as binding the Minister's statement, the Board, in my opinion, did not do something it was not empowered to do. Put differently, having regard to its statutory mandate, the Board clearly was not in law bound by the policy statement but on the facts of this case committed no jurisdictional error in deciding it was bound. (96)

Although it was recognized that the result may have the effect of pre-judging the population issue, the Court concluded that the Board could decide what "weight" should be given to these statements. Leave to appeal this aspect of the Barrie decision was denied so this _ratio_ still would apply to the OMB today as good law. However, it leaves the issue of the obligation of the Board to apply government policy rife with ambiguity.

In further considering the question of jurisdiction, the Court referred to the decision of the Court of Appeal in Cedarvale Tree Services Ltd. and Labourers Int'l Union of North America, Local 183, (97)

> ...the Board is master of its own house not only as to all questions of fact and law falling within the ambit of the jurisdiction conferred upon it by the Act, but with respect to all questions of procedure when acting within that jurisdiction. In my view, the only rule which should be stated by the Court (if it be a rule at all) is that the Board should, when its jurisdiction is questioned, adopt such procedures as appear to it to be just and convenient in the particular circumstances in the case before it."

> It is also clear law that such a tribunal is not required to bring its proceedings to a halt merely because it has been served with a notice of motion for an order of _certiorari_ or prohibition. It is entitled, if it thinks fit, to carry its pending proceedings forward until such time as order of the Court has

actually been made prohibiting its further activity or quashing some order already made by which it assumed jurisdiction.

To summarize, the implications of Justice Robins' view is that as long as the Board is acting within its jurisdiction, it is for the Board to determine the "weight" to be given to evidence placed before it. Moreover, the OMB is not bound in law by government policy statements.

The Board resumed its hearings on the Barrie Annexation issue the day after the Divisional Court decision was orally delivered. They immediately reiterated their position that evidence contrary to the Minister's letter could not be led and that the Board was not obligated to allow for cross-examination of the the policy statement. The hearings were eventually completed, and the decision rendered by the Board on October 5, 1977. (98) The annexation order was issued shortly thereafter.

An appeal of the decision was launched by the Township of Innisfil on the cross-examination issue. When a favourable decision was handed down in favour of Innisfil Township by the Divisional Court(99), the City of Barrie went to the Ontario Court of Appeal. (100) The decision that was handed down ultimately handed down by the Court of Appeal confirmed the findings of the Cloverdale case(101). Speaking for the Court on this matter, Lacourciere J.A. said this:

> With respect to the Board's refusal to permit cross-examination on the question of the Government's policy on the population issue, I am satisfied that this did not constitute an error of law. ... I agree

with Robins, J., in his reasons delivered on the judicial review application that "having regard to its statutory mandate, the Board clearly was not in law bound by the policy statement...." In other words, the Board did have a discretion whether to adopt and how best to implement Government policy in the area of population. This is not to say that the Board would be wrong in feeling obliged, at a later stage, to follow Government policy, particularly when dealing with a specific policy, as stated in this case, in contrast to a general policy. (102)

The court went on to adopt the passage by J. A. Kennedy in Re Township of Caledon Official Plan cited above(103) as the desirable approach for the OMB to take on government policy. However, no attempt was made to confine or structure the discretion granted to the OMB under any legislation in Ontario or Canada.

The matter as to whether or not a Minister could be cross-examined on the policy statement issued by his office or cabinet eventually went to the Supreme Court of Canada. Estey J. held that the provisions of the existing Planning Act (104), the Statutory Powers Procedure Act (105), and enabling legislation for the OMB (106) did not singlely or in combination require the Board to follow government policy:

A court will require the clearest statutory direction along the lines, for example, of the Broadcasting Act, (R.S.C. 1970. c.B-11, s,27(1)) to enable the executive branch of Government to give binding policy directions to an administrative tribunal and to make such directions immune from challenge by cross-examination or otherwise by the objectors. (107)

Since Estey J. could not find evidence of any obligation on the Board to receive a letter from the Minister under any of the above statutes, the evidence should be regarded as ordinary communication between the Board and the Minister. No doubt the desire to give such policy statements more official weight was behind the new provision in subsection 3(5) of the Planning Act, 1983. However, we might well ask whether the phrase "shall have regard to" is sufficiently clear and forceful to achieve the goals of programmes and policies such as ALC.

In the result, the OMB had no right to curtail the rights of citizens to object to government policies. However, the Barrie Annexation case also squarely stated that the discretionary capacity of the Board must be maintained in the face of a strong government policy statement.

The upshot is that prediction of the application of policies on decisions involving controversial issues is a difficult and risky business. The implications of this discretionary power for matters such as ALC suggest considerable flexibility is a detriment. This assertion is borne out in the examination of the OMB's record over the past decade as reflected in certain decisions rendered on the application of provincial policies on ALC. Consequently it is to a survey of these policies and their interpretation that this analysis now must turn.

The Application of the Food Land Guidelines.

As a result of public pressure to prevent the decline of Ontario's agricultural land stock in the 1960s and 1970s and the growth of interest in environmental matters(108), the provincial government tabled the Food Land Guidelines(109) in 1978. It is necessary to examine this policy statement, briefly consider its impact on land use planning in Ontario and then review some of the major decisions that the OMB has rendered on interpretation and application of them here.

The _Food Land Guidelines_ represent an innovative attempt by the provincial government to structure and control decentralized planning decisions. They require a municipality to identify lands with agricultural potential, to rate them in order of priority and to evaluate impacts that would be generated by alternative uses of the lands. In addition, the municipality must justify any proposed non-agricultural use in terms of need, prior servicing commitments and the logical extension of an existing community. Thus, the _Guidelines_ may be regarded as an inventory of the various factors a municipality must consider in deciding how and to what extent to protect agricultural land.

Relative to other ALC programmes in North America, the Ontario system is regarded as one of the most decentralized. (110) This is suggested by Table 3 and Figure 3, which show that other jurisdictions employ two or even three-tier parallel structures. For example, under the Quebec system supported by aggressive policy implementation by the Parti Quebecois, two separate parallel structures are involved. (111) Accordingly, both a specialized agricultural zoning statute (112) and an administrative tribunal, the Commission de Protection du Territoire Agricole du Quebec (CPTAQ), now shape the centralized ALC program. As Glenn observes, the result has been a more vigorous conservation program than that presently evident in

Ontario.

The impact of the _Guidelines_ on planning practices and OMB decision-making is illustrated through consideration of two decisions that have generated considerable rancour in Ontario: the series of decisions on the plan for urbanization in the Regional Municipality of Niagara rendered in the late 1970s and the 1985 OMB decision on agricultural land preservation in Brampton.

1) Urbanization in the Niagara Region.

The unique combination of rich soils and moderate climate in the Niagara region make it one of the most important areas for growing peaches and other tender fruits in Canada. (114) However, in the early 1960s it became apparent that this bounty could not be protected without more centralized government action. To promote the development of a localized response to this problem, the Ontario government enacted legislation to encourage regional planning. (115)

Approximately ten regional governments have been formed in southern Ontario since that legislation was first passed(115a). The first of these was the Regional Municipality of Niagara, which was created in 1969 and given a mandate to produce a land use plan within four years. When this land use plan was finally produced, it launched a flood of litigation and a series of OMB hearings on the issue of ALC. First adopted by regional council for the Municipality of Niagara on December 20, 1973, (116) it was submitted to the Minister for approval later the same month in an incomplete form. Additional details, including urban area boundary maps, were not forwarded until mid-1974.

.The plan itself was a mixture of contradictions and the response to it should have been predicted. For example, among the policies and objectives of the plan were ones which sought to preserve good agricultural land on the one hand and to maximize the use of existing municipal services and to honour commitments to municipalities for expanding their urban land base on the other. Regarding the former objective, the proposed plan sought to use good agricultural land for urban expansion only when necessary so as to afford maximum protection to tender fruit and grape lands in the region.

In their response, the Ontario government's disillusionment with this attempt to generate local support for ALC was apparent. The Minister responsible advised the regional council that the suggested boundaries were unacceptable and requested changes. However, the revised boundaries were also rejected and on February 16, 1977 the Minister told the council that Cabinet had decided to reduce the proposed urban areas by an additional 3,000 acres. (117)

The result of the Cabinet decision was that over seventy-four referrals related to the plan were made. This effectively prevented implementation of the Cabinet decision. Of the 74 referrals, 51 were requested by land owners or municipalities who objected to the decision because certain areas had been excluded from the designated urban areas. The balance of the requests were made by the Preservation of Agricultural Lands Society (PALS) or persons affiliated with that organization. They sought further reductions in the urban areas.

The OMB responded to this enormous number of referrals by dividing them into two groups, which were heard separately in 1978 and 1980. These hearings attracted wide public and media attention and resulted in numerous stories in the electronic and print media and the production of a film by the National Film Board of Canada. (117a)

The first hearing dealt with 15 referrals relating to land south of the Niagara Escarpment. The OMB decision was generally in favour of further reductions in the urban areas surrounding Thorald and Niagara Falls. In reaching its decision, the Board weighed the policies contained in the regional plan, although the plan had not been approved by the Minister, and concluded that the region had overestimated its housing needs. (118)

The approach taken by the OMB led to an application for a rehearing by two developers. (119) These developers owned land that was part of the largest parcel excluded by the Board. Since it had been included in the areas approved by Cabinet in the February 1977 decision, they argued that the OMB decision should be considered void. The rehearing was denied and subsequent applications to Divisional Court for a review of the rehearing decision and a judicial review of the OMB decision (120) were also dismissed. In addition, four petitions of the OMB decision were made to Cabinet. Two of these were subsequently withdrawn and the Cabinet reaffirmed the OMB's decision with regard to the other two petitions. (121)

By the time the OMB heard the testimony on the second set of referrals, the Food Land Guidelines had been released. The statement of government policy included the following passage:

> Except in circumstances where the Provincial Government decides that an important agricultural resource is involved, the Foodland Guidelines would not be applied to lands that have been designated for urban use in previously approved official plans or approved zoning by-laws which implement such plans. (122)

This statement had a bearing on the OMB's approach to the remaining referrals in the second decision, Re Niagara Planning Area Official Plan, No. 2. (123) In this decision, the Board did an about-face on the housing needs issue, concluding that the region had not overestimated housing needs to the extent that the first decision had indicaed. Moreover, the Board accepted the generous boundaries that were provided in the plan approved by Cabinet.

On the contentious issue of consents to sever, the OMB was much less accomodating. The Board noted that the only policy on consents in the proposed plan concerned unique agricultural land and this was inadequate in view of the Guidelines. (123) Accordingly, the OMB modified the consent policy to conform with the Guidelines and specified that consents were not to be granted for retirement lots or for lots for family members. Regarding the latter aspect of consents, intervenors at the hearings had observed that these lots were often transferred after a short period of time. (124) Not surprisingly, this decision on consents was the subject of a petition to Cabinet, and the OMB's strict interpretation of the Guidelines was varied to allow the creation of the retirement and family lots in limited "hardship" cases.

The other major issue that the Board considered was the permanency of the proposed urban boundaries. According to the Guidelines

> The boundary designation should be refined to show definite staging in 5 to 10 year intervals or time contours which will indicate the direction and extent of future urban growth, the rate at which it will occur, and the time limits within which agriculture can occupy the area as an interim use. (125)

The intent of this provision is to reduce land speculation and fragmentation of land parcels in anticipation of future land use conflicts. It has been noted that this anticipation often leads to a lessening of agricultural productivity in the lands immediately surrounding urban centres. (126)

In Re Niagara, the boundary issue provided a particularly graphic example of the difficulties this provision was intended to address. The urban boundaries proposed in the regional plan were not considered permanent since they could be modified at a future date. However, the Guidelines suggested boundaries which abutted prime agricultural land should be "as permanent as possible". (127) Thus, the Board added an appendix to the plan which stipulated that this in fact should be the policy of the region. In the result, it would appear that the OMB was more lenient with respect to ALC in the second decision. Among the possible explanations for this shift was the fact that the composition of the Board was different for each hearing and the majority of individual referrals at the second hearing were requests for inclusion in urban areas, whereas two-thirds of the individual referrals for the first hearing were requests for exclusion of farmland from urban areas.(128)

The aftermath of this extensive process is effectively shown in the "before and after" maps presented in Figure 4. What these maps show is that very little actually changed as a consequence of the extensive interventions made by PALS and the publication of the Guidelines. Public dismay with these results was reflected in a series of editorials offered in the Toronto Star and The Globe and Mail and the numerous "Letters to the Editor" in both papers writtten in response to the Cabinet and OMB decisions.(129)

Gayler (130) has studied the OMB decisions on ALC in the Niagara region and he traces the difficulties that were encountered to uncertainty in the regional planning process:

> During the 1970s it became clear that earlier forecasts of population increase and urban expansion in the Niagara region were too great. There has been a steady decline in the national birth rate since the 1950s and a decline locally in the rate of net in-migration. Moreover, a worsening economic climate, increasing development costs, and greater planning restrictions have led to a decline in the rate of land conversion from rural to urban uses. These changing circumstances afford an opportunity to plan for more compact urban areas and thus protect the area's valuable agricultural land. However, attempts of achieve these ends have been constantly frustrated by a regional and local planning process which has been loath to recognize such

a conservationist cause or the need to plan for slower growth.

Gaylor goes on to explore some specific issues which he claims contributed to the conflict at the OMB hearings over the Niagara plan. Foremost among these issues are the difficulties in accurately forecasting urban growth and desire on the part of minicipalities to provide ample space for future residential and industrial developments. However, political attitudes towads urban expansion were the key explanation for the intransigience of the Niagara regional government. (131)

2) The Re_Brampton Decision

A more recent decision of the OMB on the application of the Guidelines considered the problem of ALC in the context of the Brampton official plan. (132) It follows on the heals of an ALC decision on a tract in the adjacent Peel Region municipality of Mississauga called the "hole-in-the-doughnut" rendered by the Board in 1981. (133) In that case, 12,000 acres of class-one agricultural land were approved for development and this land in now being gobbled up. The Re_Brampton decision produced mixed results; not all of the land sought was approved but more than 5,500 acres of prime land north of the City could eventually be developed.

The result in the Re_Brampton decision was a major disappointment for the APPEAL intervenors. Their hopes had been raised by a favourable decision of the OMB the year before in Re Caledon Official_Plan Amendment 38. (134) In that decision the

Board held no justification had been demonstrated for the residential and industrial uses proposed. Since the required studies contemplated by the approved official plan for amendments to demonstrate need had not been prepared in compliance with the Guidelines, the Board viewed the Caledon proposal as "premature."

The official plan under consideration for the city of Re Brampton sought approval of nearly 7,000 acres of land for industrial and residential purposes. Although the OMB disallowed a bid for industrialization of 600 hectares on the west side of Brampton, it rejected most of the referrals directed to it by the Association of Peel People Evaluating Land (APPEAL). In contast the OMB did accept most of the submissions directed to it from the Ministry of Agriculture and Food (MAF). (135)

In the Brampton case, APPEAL also argued that the need for the designated land had not been demonstrated. However, the planners and developers seem to have carried the day. Municipal officials argued that a large stock of affordable housing is necessary to attract industry to the City. Since Brampton is located conveniently for both commuters and industry and the city has serviced lots under the South Peel Servicing Scheme, the potential for expansion is enormous.

Like the second decision of the Board on the Niagara fruitbelt lands, here the panel recognized the dual need to generate a long-term plan and consolidate existing official plan policiesin one document. They noted that past experience with urbanization forces were a key motivating factors "because

Brampton through the 1960s and 1970s, experienced very rapid growth."(136) The Board went on to observe that it accepted the premise of the municipality that what was required was a long-term document which would be valid "over a period of atleast 20 years."(137)

The Board's decision(138) is a particularly strong endorsement of the role of the free market in determining both housing mix and the pace of development:

> The board has no reason on the evidence to doubt that the maximum densities provided for ... reflect the present preferences of the housing market, at least roughly. The evidence showed that the housing market can and does change. If the market turns towards higher densities we can be sure that developers will not be deferred .... They will undoubtedly apply for any necessary amendment to the table, and will be in a position to... lessen future development pressures on prime agricultural land.
>
> The board is also certain that if a trend does develop in the market towards higher densities, the city will not be slow to recognize it, and will ... as necessary attempt to accommodate it.
>
> The philosophy of all the following is that, in a competitive regional market like the Toronto-centred region there is nothing the city can do, even in the name of preserving prime agricultural land, to compel developers to build housing of types or densities the developers know cannot be sold.(Emphasis added)

The last paragraph is a particularly strong endorsement of the importance of the marketplace in shaping land use policies in Ontario. However, this type of philosophy brings into question the existence of the OMB as an agency of government intended to regulate land use. Clearly a body such as the OMB was established for this purpose and it must take a role in shaping new attitudes to housing density. Recognizing the limitations of the marketplace with respect to issues like ALC seems like a good place to start.

Other themes which emerge from the Board decision in Re Brampton are the inevitability of development and the desirability of exaggerated, almost explosive, population growth.(139) Both themes underlie the following provisions in the Brampton Official Plan dealing with growth:

Anticipating and Managing Growth.

In the 1970's, Brampton sustained one of the highest rates in Southern Ontario. The 1979 Assessments Census figure of 129,000 represents a doubling of population in less than ten years.

In the future, efforts will be made to control the growth rate relative to the City's financial ability to provide an approved standard of services. Conversely, the provision of public services will be directed towards the achievement of the financial and other objectives of the Plan.

The population capacity within the new urban boundary ... is in the order of 335,000 and for the City as a whole is 344,000.

The projection of a 4 per cent growth rate, compounded, results in a 25-year time frame for the Plan.

The employment activity rate is expected to rise to almost 50 per cent resulting in a total of 170,000 jobs in Brampton when the Plan matures. The proportion of retail and service jobs compared with manufacturing jobs is expected to increase from 45 percent in 1979 to 55 per cent at the turn of the century.

In the short term it is expected, that by 1986, the population of the City will reach 176,000 and employment opportunities will total 80,400.(140)

This section was challenged by APPEAL on the grounds that "it fails to recognize the high soil and climatic capability of Brampton for agriculture and does not address the preservation of agricultural lands."(141) However, the Board rejected the referral because APPEAL had not set out specific alternative population growth and economic expansion rates along with a different time-frame. Thus, the Board specifically exercized its discretion in favour of the proposition offered by the City of Brampton that the growth which is anticipated in the region is inevitable.

Related to this issue is another which must be highlighted here -- residential density. (142) Arguably, the strength of APPEAL's case for ALC rested largely on their contention "that the possibility of increasing densities of urban growth to lessen pressures for the use of prime food lands has not been "studied", as required by s.4C.5(5) of the Food Land Guidelines."(143) In essence, APPEAL requested that densities be increased in the areas adjacent to the urbanized part of Brampton from approximately between 7-11 units per acre to at least 13 units from one. Although the Board accepted the proposition that higher density consumes less land as self-evident, it was unwilling to accede to APPEAL's demand and would not direct a study on the question. Instead, the OMB deferred to the market and the City of Brampton's planning estimates as the guiding forces in shaping their decision in this case.

The largest area approved for development by the OMB in this new urban boundary was a 4,000 acre chunk called the Ronto-Sandringham lands. The size of the new area in proportion to the curent size of Brampton is remarkable as Figure 6 shows. This parcel abutts the northern edge of Bramlea and it is owned by large investors such as George Wimpey Canada Ltd., Shell Canada Ltd. and the Ronto Development Corporations. (144) It has been estimated that the area could provide housing for approximately 70,000 people if the Liberal Cabinet agrees with the Re Brampton decision. However, this seems unlikely in view of recent opinions expressed by Jack Riddell on the decision in November 1985 and the subsequent new policy promulgated by the Liberal government in response to the OMB decision.

This approach to urban boundary determination in Re Brampton is interesting for several reasons. As pointed out above already, most of the area that has been approved for development is now actively being farmed. Thus, it would seem that only a very strong case would seem to justify this kind of designation of mainly class-one land. Another recent OMB decision held that only a strong need could justify this kind of erosion of rural boundaries.

The policy argument underlying APPEAL's position in Brampton was stated by Verna Flowers, the driving force behind the group, to the media after the OMB decision was released on October 31, 1985:

> With a growing population there will be a need for more food... It makes more sense economically to grow food on good land such as this. Farmers are going

broke on poor land. (145)

Although the OMB did not address this policy matter explicitly in Re Brampton, it is clear that this was not viewed as a persuasive argument for ALC and rejecting the city demand for the land "needed" for residential development. APPEAL desired that the OMB would reflect its mandate to regulate rather than promote development and defer to the marketplace.

Frustration with this type of long-term perspective on the preservation of Ontario food lands is mounting among planners and municipal officials in cities such as Brampton. John Marshall was extremely critical of APPEAL's efforts in Re Brampton, stating that

> They don't care about jobs or growth or housing, they just care about land and somebody else has to worry about where people are going to live. (146)

Marshall has pointed out that this land could be under development as early as 1988 if the new boundary for the City is approved by Cabinet.

To conclude, it is apparent that the OMB's approach to ALC under the Guidelines was extremely unpredictable and generally unsatisfactory. The decisions, when taken collectively, suggest a pro-development bias and general tendency for the Board to either reproduce market conditions in their policies on ALC or defer to the market. These results also suggest that the OMB may not be the best body to deal with this type of problem.

The Foodland Preservation Statement: Tougher Measures?

The Re Brampton decision set in motion a process that led to the release of a document titled Foodland Preservation by the Ministry of Food and Agriculture in February 1986. (147) As critic for this portfolio while he was in the Liberal opposition, the new Minister, Jack Riddell, urged that the Guidelines be toughened to protect areas such as Brampton. The OMB decision no doubt was a source of embarrassment for Mr. Riddell and this may explain why this draft document was released as soon after Re Brampton as it was.

The new draft policy statement deals with two main problems perceived in the operation of the Guidelines. These problems, which will be examined below in turn, are: a) Municipal Growth Forecasting, and b) Severances. Prior to examining these two aspects of the new statement, however, some general comments should be directed at the document.

The first of these general comments is that the new statement appears to have weakened the emphasis on goals, when compared with the Guidelines. Although this may be attributed in part to the fact that the new statement is more concise, the overall effect of this change may be to erode the value of new policy statement.

Counterbalancing the lack of emphasis on goals are three specific provisions which state provincial policy fairly explicitly:

1.1.1   Prime agricultural land as defined be placed in an
         agricultural designation and be clearly identified in
         the official plan and on the land use schedule

1.1.2   The agricultural designation be as large as practical
         and consist of predominantly prime agricultural land

1.1.3   The agricultural designation be continuous and uninterrupted
         by non-agricultural designations which permit land uses
         incompatible with agriculture. (148)

After setting out these important policies on designation, which
are not substantially different from those in the Guidelines,
Foodland Preservation goes on to describe the approach that
municipalities should take to land use conflicts, severances and
other matters. However, it is apparent that these policies still
grant an individual municipality enormous discretionary authority
over their ultimate approach to ALC. The only way the Minister
of Agriculture can ensure these policies receive priority is
through intervention in OMB hearings or threatening to take
action against the municipalities.

Another potential weakness in the new policy statement is
that the requirement for inventories of specialized agricultural
area as provided in several sections of the Guidelines (149) has
been dropped. Moreover, the requirement for mapping of the
agricultural land base and for including a priority rating of the
mapped land is also absent from the new statement. The explicit
policy rationale for this alteration is unclear but it likely
would include factors such as declining funds to pursue such
research. One of the difficulties this might pose is that it
would become difficult to assess the environmental impact of
urban developments if such mapping is not continued.

Other weaknesses include the provisions on the desgination of sites for mineral removal and the overall trend in the document to defer to municipalities and the Ministry of Natural Resources on the identification of sites for aggregate and other materials.(150) However, these are relatively minor matters relative to the major ones that concern this analysis.

1) The Objectives of the New Policy

Having now set out some of the weaknesses in the document, we can now turn to a brief exposition of the two major objectives of the new policy statement.

a) Municipal Growth Forecasting.

One of the key provisions that the new policy statement attempts to address is the problem posed by current approaches to municipal growth forecasting. According to the new policy, use of prime farmland for non-agricultural purposes "would only be permitted if the need to use this land is justified, and such justification is documented."(151) In addition the new statement suggests that municipalities will not be able to earmark prime farmland for urban development unless that development is likely to occur within 10 years. (152) Such a provision would have prevented the large land annexation of land approved in Re Brampton.

b) Severances and Nuisance Actions.

Another proposal in the new policy statement concerns severances. Under the Guidelines a farmer can sever lots to children if they are working on the farm or reserve a small portion of his lot for future retirement. As the economic situation of farmers has worsened, studies have shown that some are severing small properties from their farms and effectively marketing them; a rapid turn-over of less than 2 years is the estimated to be average rate of time before conveyance. Although the Board has held that it will not allow such severances to relieve economic hardship and will not allow premature severances to children (153), it has been reluctant to prevent farmers from setting aside land for retirement planning. A Board decision made in 1980 held that a farmer could sever even if he fully intended to later sell the property and move to Florida.(154) Brooks stated for the Board that

> ...a retirement lot does not "become" a non-farm lot -- it is from the start a non-farm lot. A farmer living on his retirement lot is perfectly entitled to decide at any time that, after all, he would rather live out his retirement years in Hamilton, or Florida, and thereupon sell the lot to anyone at all who will buy. This risk is unknowingly assumed by the municipalities that adopt Official Plan provisions contemplating the creation of retirement lots of this sort.(155)

What Brooks did not go on to point out is that this policy can generate problems for farmers on adjacent properties because the severed lots are often purchased by urbanites. (156) These urbanites have been launching nuisance actions against the farmers, protesting the unseemly noises and smells that accompany modern industrial agricultural practices.

The new policy would ban farmers from severing these small properties on their lots in most circumstances and encourage municipalities to promote retirement in nearby villages and life-leases. It does not rule out severances entirely but stipulates strong prerequisites for future municipal planning. (157) However, the policy has met with strong opposition from farmers and no doubt could be challenged under section 15 of the Charter of Rights and Freedoms as discriminatory. It seems more likely the province will attempt to deal with this problem through "Right to Farm" legislation. A Committee is currently touring southern Ontario and hearing testimony on the problem and will likely report later this spring. (158) Nevertheless, this is a difficult problem and a solution will not likely be quickly forthcoming.

2) Some Unresolved Issues.

At this point, the discussion shifts ground to consider some of the matters raised in the OMB decisions that seem largely unresolved despite the intent of the new policy statement. These have been identified as a) determination of need by the OMB; b) threshold of farmland viability; and, c) structuring OMB discretion. In the balance of this section, these matters will receive consideration.

a) The Documentation of 'Need': More than Hearsay
   But Less than Science.

The key issue which still remains unresolved despite the new policy statement is what kind of documentation is required to demonstrate "need" for development. As we have seen already, this was the controversial issue in most of the OMB decisions rendered on the provisions in the Guidelines between 1978 and 1985. (159)

The OMB approach to the question of need in Re Caledon suggests that, as a minimum, the preparation of a market study or report is a prerequisite to approval of plans to develop agricultural lands. The Board held that in view of the Guidelines

> some detailed or qualified study should have been done to indicate the need or demand for urban development of these lands. No market study was requested or prepared. Partial or no development would mean loss of lands given priority in the plan for agricultural use in favour of a use whose fulfillment and desired financial benefits may never occur. The only evidence of demand is from Mr. Black [town planner] who indicated he had received five telephone inquiries in the last two years regarding industrial land in the area. (160)

The question of need was also a crucial issue in the Re Brampton case. One of the intervenors who made a statement on the issue to the Board was the current Minister of Agriculture, Jack Riddell, who was Liberal critic for the portfolio at the time. Riddell argued that the population forecasts upon which the need for the land was based were misleading. In response, the Board(161) said this:

> The question of population forecasts was exhaustively investigated during the hearing. Forecasts are, of course, subject to error, but the board is convinced that the target population estimate of 344,000 persons was not just "picked out of the air" - _it was very carefully calculated. Since justification of need, pursuant to the Food Land Guidelines, must involve forecasting, local planning authorities have no option but to attempt to ensure that the forecast is done prudently and with professional impartiality._ The board is satisfied, so far as the target population prediction is concerned, that the evidence it heard meets this test. (Emphasis added)

Despite these comments in Re Caledon and Re Brampton, it is still unclear what exactly the municipalities such as Brampton must show to demonstrate "need." Is it enough to have a single consultant report prepared by a "professional"? This raises question of agency and the likelihood that municipalities will hire those consultants who share their biases. Perhaps this problem could be partially overcome if intervenor groups such as APPEAL and PALS were given funding to prepare their own scenarios.

Whether a municipality should sponsor more than one needs study in this era of fiscal restraint is a moot point. Moreover, two reports could produce absolutely contradictory opinions and require further evaluation. The preferred alternative would be to expand the planning provisions in legislation such as the Environmental Assessment Act (162) to require a greater range of options for their communities than the traditional high growth forecasts that are usually presented. At a minimum the onus should be on the municipalities to show need in terms of a number of alternative futures for the community. Thus, need should be estimated for no-growth, low growth, medium growth and high growth scenarios. To allow a community such as Brampton to employ a high growth scenario as its desired alternate future to estimate need for residential and industrial areas without adequate justification seems a clear violation of good planning practice. (163)

b) Threshold of Farmland Viability.

Another issue arising out of the recent decisions of the OMB on ALC may be termed "the threshold of farmland viability" test that has been applied. In brief, such a test is implicit in the Re Brampton decision.

Evidence that such a test is being employed by the Board, both consciously and unconsciously, is found in other recent decisions on the Guidelines. For example, in Re Mississauga,(164) the OMB regarded the class-one land under consideration as virtually surrounded. Urban development of this land was deemed inevitable, especially in view of market pressures.

The Board distinguished Re Mississauga in Re Caledon when the former decision was cited as a precedent by counsel for the Town of Caledon, stating

It is clear that the circumstances there were very different from the present case... This matter presents the reverse circumstances of an area of high capability land, much of which is still actively farmed, surrounded on three sides by operating farms. (165)

This text suggest that an important part of this test is whether land is actually being farmed. The difficulty with such an emphasis is the fact that land speculators may actually discourage farming on their investments to ensure quicker sub-division approval.

c) Structuring OMB Discretion.

The problem of ALC suggests a need for the OMB and other planning bodies to begin to structure their exercise of discretion. (166) In the past, administrative tribunals have developed their policies on a case-by-case basis.

This approach to policy development has been criticized by scholars such as Davis (167) because it allows the tribunals to escape accountability for their decisions. Moreover, those affected by the exercise of authority have often put forward arguments that the main defects with abuse of discretion if the decision-making capacities of administrative tribunals were structured. (168)

How might a "structured" discretionary process operate to promote ALC? An example is provided by the 1983 Board decision, Re Richmond Hill (169) wherein it was held that estate residential development would act to constrain the northward push of urban development in Richmond Hill. The town had proposed a designation which allowed large estate homes, maintained permanent recreational uses and recognized existing agricultural uses to create an urban fringe. Such an approach will hopefully act to preserve agricultural lands in the fringe surrounding this Town.

Although this is a unique case because of the peculiar landscape, it could provide a basis for approval of urban boundaries in official plans that must deal with ALC. Certainly, it would be a fairly accurate reflection of the intent of the Guidelines and the new Foodlands Preservation documents to do so. Moreover the Board has expressed support for municipal plans which do just this.

This is only one example of the kind of changes that could be made. Others could be devised based on the deficiencies identified above. Clearly advocates of ALC would applaud such a move because they would know what contested ground was and they could focus their energies.

Developers would probably also applaud some kind of structuring of discretion. This conclusion is supported by the following observation in the 1981 report from the Economic Council of Canada, Reforming Regulation (170):

>   heme that emerged from the
> Perhaps the strongest t
> case studies and interviews was that what businessmen
> found objectionable was not the regulations themselves
> but the process by which they were introduced, made
> known, and applied. For in pursuing their statutory
> responsibilities governments often use fairly broad,

blanket legislation or regulations, leaving considerable administrative responsibilities to officials. How that discretionary power is to be used, or how it is to be related to the regulatory activities of other agencies, is not always prescribed. The scope for decisions that are perceived as less than evenhanded is quite wide, and it is not surprising that businessmen, who tend to regard government as a somewhat monolithic structure, naturally view this with growing irritation. They worry that uneven application or enforcement may give an advantage to competitors. Most of the businessmen interviewed also recognized that regulatory consistency does not necessarily mean equal enforcement of identical standards everywhere, and that the application of regulations should be sufficiently flexible to take account of local conditions. The desire for consistency is not incompatible with that for flexibility, but it requires a fine balance of judgment and a willingness to respond on both sides. (Emphasis added)

Thus a more predicable investment climate would probably be welcomed by businessmen even though one can anticipate considerable rancour over restrictions which would prohibit aggressive development and discourage land speculation on the rural-urban fringe of Ontario.

Whether or not the approach taken in Re Richmond Hill succeeds, it could become a precedent if the Board was encouraged to structure its discretion. The process could be initiated through an amendment to the enabling legislation of the OMB, or through less formal mechanisms until the required changes could be drafted. The intent would be to allow the Board to express its intent to take a more favourable approach to ALC. Accordingly, the OMB would expect a municipality to create such a designation where prime agricultural land was threatened.

The advantage of such a structuring of discretion is that it would send a clear signal to municipalities, land speculators and farmers. Such a message is needed in view of the record on implementation of the Guidelines over the past decade.

The potential for structuring the rule-making of bodies such as the OMB would probably be restrained by the common law, however. (171) According to this argument, tribunals in Canada are confined to taking into account only those things which they have the legislative mandate to consider. What is taken into account becomes part of the exercise of discretionary powers. Thus, to begin to structure discretion so as to refuse to take into account or neglect to take into account matters which might seem irrelevant to the OMB on an issue such as ALC would probably be regarded by the courts as an abuse of discretion.

At the same time, it is noteworthy that rule making by administrative agencies has received both legislative and judicial support in some common law jurisdictions. For example, in the United States agencies publish proposed rules and invite public comment on them. The comments are then used to revise the rules, and any protests are directed to a final version of the rules.

Whether such a model of rule-making could be employed by the OMB in relation to ALC is unclear. However, such an approach might be a more satisfactory alternative to the current discretionary approah now mandated under section 3 of the Planning Act, 1983. It is recommended, therefore, that the OMB be given the power to make pospective rules on ALC based on the new Foodland Guidelines and be required to seek public input into such rule making. Through such a process, those with a vested interest in the formulation of the rules associated with ALC would then be able to predict the outcome of offiial plan referrals such as Re Brampton and Re Caledon with greater certainty. This might make the decisions rendered more acceptable to all the parties involved in the process of ALC because it would give the appearance of greater justice.

In the alternative, if these kinds of issues cannot be resolved in a satisfactory way while the Board retains jurisdiction over ALC related matters, it may be necessary to restructure it to reduce some of its independence from the government. Such a change would no doubt erode, if not completely undermine, the roles of insulator and adjudicator played by the Board currently but this may be price we have to pay to conserve agricultural land in Ontario. Moreover, it would make ALC a clear electoral matter rather than an issue on the fringes of regulation, legitimated by decisions from a quasi-judicial, pro-development organ.

Structural Barriers

Even if the problems that have been encountered in trying to encourage municipalities to engage in planning more sensitive to ALC can be overcome and the members of the OMB undergo a paradigm shift with respect to the issue, key sources of the problems faced by farmers in Canada will probably not disappear. Thus, the _Food Land Guidelines_ and _Foodlands Preservation_ policy statements should not be viewed as an end in themselves. Problems related to ALC have deep roots and it is apparent that many structural barriers to reform are not being addressed. Some of the barriers considered in the folowing subsections below include: 1) The Jurisdictional Dilemma; 2) Farm-Generated Responses; and 3) Strengthening Vertical Linkages. However, others could be identified as well. The embryonic argument offered is that these barriers are as important as those already being examined by the Ontario government in the new policy on ALC.

1) The Jurisdictional Dilemma

The _Re Brampton_ decision and other OMB decisions show that all levels of government have a stake in agricultural land conservation and a role to play in shaping the ultimate future course of land-use policy in Ontario. The complexities of subsidies, soil erosion, urban encroachment and other issues which have a bearing on agricultural land conservation suggest that solutions can only be developed through cooperation between various levels of government.

Undoubtedly, jurisdictional blocks are the most serious long-term threat to ALC. The municipalities are primarily "creatures of the provinces" and despite calls to recognize their need for entrenched powers, remain bound by doctrines that apply to corporations regarding their _vires_. (172) Since the municipalities are not recognized in the constitution, their ability to undertake activities such as down-zoning land and implementation of programs to conserve land are limited. (173)

Another jurisdictional block is the current arrangements in the constitution regarding environmental matters. (174) Constitutionally, agriculture is a responsibility shared between the provincial and federal governments. Adding to this confusion is the fact that major decisions on land use in Ontario are made by regional and municipal governments. In the 1960s and 1970s the Province made a gallant effort to transfer greater powers over areas such as welfare administration and social planning to these low tier governments but their efforts were largely unsuccessful.

This pattern of decentralization has been questioned recently and it is apparent that a retreat from decentralization is currently underway. The Economic Council of Canada described the retreat as follows:

> where earlier the provinces were prepared to divest substantial regulatory power to municipalities, the trend has reversed, and the number of provincial statutory and regulatory land-use instruments has been increasing. This has been partly in response to heightened public concern for environmental and esthetic considerations and partly in an attempt to resolve differences between adjoining municipalities. (175)

The Council goes on to point out that this concentration of powers in the hands of the province has not served to reduce the jurisdictional and land use conflicts that the regional administrations were originally set up to address. (176) Thus, issues such as the provision of park sites, the standard of municipal service installations required of developers and ALC are being addressed by municipal councils in quite different ways.

The problem is complicated by the financial situation faced by many municipalities in southern Ontario. Most of these municipalities are seen to be poor and require urban development to bring in taxes and other revenues for service provision. The gravity of the problems faced by municipalities was recently stressed in a report prepared for the Macdonald Commission. (176) Moreover, a recent policy document issued by the Ontario government (177) stresses the need for financial impact analysis in looking at the proposals made to municipalities to develop residential and industrial siting areas.

Ultimately, more concerted action to promote ALC in Ontario will probably necessitate duplication of effort and inefficiency. While land use management is clearly a provincial responsibility, experience over the past two decades shows that the province is not doing the job. An argument that would seem to follow is that the role of the federal government should be expanded. After all, Ottawa has more money available to it and could potentially base powers of intervention on the peace, order and good government (POGG) clause that precedes section 91 of the Constitution Act, 1867.

Whether such an argument would be upheld by the courts is unclear. However, there are other considerations which suggest no matter how involved the federal government might become, the provinces will still remain responsible for land use planning. The division of powers under the Constitution Act, 1867 stipulates that this should be the same in granting powers over natural resources to the provinces under section 92(A) and ownership of land resources under section 109.(177a) Thus, constitutional niceties such as the federal POGG power aside, provisions guarantee that ALC will remain largely a provincial responsibility. Consequently it would seem to make sense to build up the role of agencies such as the Foodlands Preservation Branch of the Ontario Ministry of Food and Agriculture through federal grants.

Rather than encouraging greater federal involvement in ALC, an alternative approach might be to establish special taxation arrangements or subsidies for municipalities directly. This would circumvent the need for federal-provincial cooperation on ALC by allowing municipalities to maintain an adequate revenue base for expanding social services and simultaneously conserve foodlands. It is noteworthy in this regard that the Macdonald Commission made recommendations to increase the financial resources available to municipalities.(178)

2) Farm-Generated Responses(179)

It is important to bear in mind that there are some positive aspects for farmers created by urban expansion. For example, the market effects offer some farmers the opportunity to reap fairly substantial windfall profits upon sale of their land to developers and there are many who are willing to benefit from such effects. In a period when farm income is falling, the promise of future windfall benefits may spur the process of land use change that eventually leads to urbanization of the area.

Thus, the role of farm-generated responses to this urbanization pressure must be taken into account. As Bryant has demonstrated, farmers vary their responses to the threat of urban expansion.(180) Their behavior will reflect perceptions of factors such as the threat of modifications, the resources available to farmers to fight the new urban residents, and the ability to adapt.

The basic framework of Bryant's work is shown in Figure 6. Bryant(181) explains the hypothesis that underlies this framework as follows:

> The key...lies in understanding the role attributed to the farmer's _anticipation_ of urban expansion. This anticipation can be interpreted as an _evaluation_ by the farmer of the potential urbanization forces in the surrounding environment, and it thus act acts as the link between the actual and level of these forces and changes in agricultural land uses and practices.(Emphasis original)

Bryant has applied this framework to the analysis of urbanization-agriculture interactions in the Paris region of France(182) while his results show that there is a strong correlation between urbanization forces and the farmer's evaluation of them, he was not able to show the link between evaluations of urban pressures and actual changes in farming practices. Bryant argues that this probably reflects an adaptive strategy on the part of farmers.

The implications of Bryant's study are two-fold. First, it is important to recognize the elements of the private land-owners decision-making capacity and the impact this has on ALC. Clearly it is not enough to preserve agricultural land if farmers in the areas adjacent to sub-divisons look forward to selling off their land to large developers for a significant profit. Secondly, attitudes towards land speculation and must be changed as much as anything to ensure that ALC takes place. Attempts to control this kind of behavior in Ontario through a special tax failed in the 1970s(183) but similar programs have operated elsewhere with success.(184) In addition, as the experience in California shows, only the farmers themselves can ultimately mount the kind of campaign necessary to protect farmland.(185) Strong incentives must be provided in order to ensure this occurs in Ontario as well. But the price of food must increase in order to do this.

3) Strengthening Vertical Linkages.

There is also a need to strengthen vertical linkages in the food supply system, as Smith has shown recently in his study of agricultural change in Quebec.(186) He maintains that the key to understanding changes in agricultural land use is a dynamic model of market interactions which takes into account the profound changes that have taken place over the last 50 years in production, distribution, retailing and consumption patterns. Smith doubts whether supply management can solve many of the weak sectors of the farm economy and prefers recent Quebec legislation which "seeks a solution to the decline evident in the food supply system by injecting capital into the processing industry."(187)

To summarize the essence of this approach, it holds that to preserve farmland, one must protect farmers. This can be accomplished through subsidization and marketing boards but such an interventionist strategy is likely to create numerous problems. In the alternative, the strategy should promote self-sufficiency in the entire food industry in Ontario and Canada by integrating all levels of production and consumption, as Figure 7 shows.

Whether the Quebec approach will succeed in its attempt to tackle the farm problem at the source remains to be seen. However, Smith's point that the structural barriers to ALC must be considered is important to keep in mind. It may very well prove impossible to generate the kind of public support necessary to decentralize urban growth, increase residential density and effectively preserve southern Ontario's foodlands as long as the importation of food grown outside of Canada continues to grow.

There are undoubtedly other structural and attitudinal barriers but these cannot be investigated here. As a final point, it is worth noting that a mixed conserver agriculture approach has been proposed as a long-term alternative to the current high-yield model of food production and this might ultimately provide the way around many of the conflicts studied in this paper in the next century.(188) However, the success of such an approach will undoubtedly turn on factors which are outside the realm conventional government; a conserver solution could only work in the context of a shift towards a new ethic about our relationship to nature and to each other as human beings. (189)

Conclusion

In the analysis above I have attempted to show that the current approach to decision-making on ALC is inadequate and that a new model should be implemented. Experience shows that municipalities cannot be relied on to ensure that ALC takes place; the financial burdens they face if they fail to promote continued economic growth are prohibitive. Thus, the province must take the lead by issuing a new policy statement which builds on the Foodlands Preservation document. This policy statement should include mechanisms to promote farmland conservation in a decentralized way but still maintain a clear central authority responsible for maintenance of a revamped ALC program.

In terms of the practices of the OMB, it is apparent that the one major shift that is necessary is the amendment of Section 3 of the Planning Act to stipulate that municipalities are bound by government policy with respect to ALC unless they can otherwise demonstrate a reason why they should not be so bound. This could be achieved by amending the wording of section 3(5) so that the phrase "shall have regard" was replaced with something more forceful. Another major component of such an amendment could be a change to in discretionary power to allow for the formulation of very basic rules on planning in the rural/urban fringe. This could include the change that was proposed above with respect to the Re Richmond Hill decision.

A revamped ALC program should also address the structural problems faced by farmers today as a means to conserve farmland. Thus, new provisions regarding inter-jurisdictional coordination and municipal financing should be devised to allow a greater number of communities in the rural/urban fringe to favour ALC without paying too great a cost. Local governments should be discouraged from favouring high population growth scenarios and low density housing in their official plans. In addition, increases in the price of food to reflect the long-term costs of current food production policies (for example, soil degradation and our current reliance on precious hydrocarbon resources) seem called.

In the alternative, it seems likely that the kind of course followed over the past decade will recur. Gradually more and more farmland in southern Ontario will be paved over and absorbed by urban-industrialism. The result will be tragic only in the eyes of the visionaries who worry about what their children's children will harvest from the tarmaced stretches in Brampton and the Niagara region. No doubt our descendants will query as to the extravagance of their ancestors in the year 2025 if they are faced with global food shortages and declining reserves of petrochemicals to produce the pesticides and fertilizers required to run their tractors. And all the social historians will be able to point to is a perception of the need for low density housing and rapid urban growth held by members of the OMB and the planning community way back in the 1980s.

Notes

* Fellow in the Faculty of Environmental Studies and Student, Osgoode Hall Law School, York University. This paper was originally prepared for the Land Use Planning Class at Osgoode in the Winter Term of 1986. The author would like to express his thanks to Professors D. Hefferon, E. Tucker and John Evans of Osgoode and D. Hoffman of the Faculty of Environmental Studies for their helpful comments and criticisms on early drafts of this paper.

1. Quoted in an editorial titled "A Vital Canadian Resource is Threatened," in the Toronto Star, Friday, Jan. 30, 1981. The editorial was the first part of a three part series that ran in the paper that week. The series, called "Our Vanishing Farmland," seems to have been scheduled during crucial testimony in an important decision on agricultural land conservation (ALC) in Ontario, the famous "hole-in-the-doughnut" decision on 12,000 acres of land in Mississauga decided by the Ontario Municipal Board in 1981. See infra, note 133 for the citation of the decision and p. 49 below for further discussion on the decision.

2. See John Hansen, "The Quality of Land Surrounding the Major Urban Centres of Canada, The United States and Britain" (1982), 11(3) Social Indicators Research 269. Hansen observes that a disproportionate amount of prime agricultural land in Canada is located adjacent to major cities compared with the U.S. and Britain. For another comparitive analysis, see F.R. Steiner and J.E. Theilacker, Protecting Farmland, (1984). Westport, Conn. : The AVI Publishing Company. [Hereinafter: Steiner and Theilacker, Protecting Farmland.]

3. Wendy L. Simpson-Lewis and Edward W. Manning, "Food for Thought: Can We Preserve Our Agricultural Land Resources?" (1981), 10 Alternatives. These authors, both senior researchers at the Lands Directorate of Environment Canada, provide a persuasive argument in favour of conservation and summarize some of the excellent work being done through this government agency. Two other recent reports on the need for sustainable agriculture in Canada are Conservation Council of Ontario, Towards a Conservation Strategy for Ontario, (1986). Toronto: Conservation Council of Ontario, and Public Advisory Committees of the Alberta Environment Commission, Prospectus for an Alberta Conservation Strategy, (1986). Edmonton: Alberta Environment. Both these reports were prepared in response to the World Conservation Strategy, a global initiative launched in 1980. For background on these two reports and the World Conservation Strategy, see D. McRobert, "Canada and the World Conservation Strategy" (1986), 21 Probe Post: Canada's Environmental Magazine. June 1986.

A general overview on sustainable production on Canadian lands (with an emphasis on agriculture) is presented in E.W. Manning, "Canada's Land: Relating Research to Reality" (1985), Paper presented to the meeting of the Gellschaft fur Kanada-Studien, Grainau, West Germany, Feb. 1985, MS. 30 pp. (Available from Lands Directorate, Environment Canada, Ottawa). Another excellent survey of the arguments for sustainable agriculture in Canada is C. Giangrande, Down to Earth: The Crisis in Canadian Farming, (1985). Toronto: House of Anansi Press. [Hereinafter: Giangrande, Down to Earth.]

4. O.J. Furuseth, "Agricultural Land Conversion: Background and Issues" (1982), 81 Journal of Geography 84. Furuseth concludes that current policies in the United States are haphazard and fail to address the causes of depletion of land in the United States. He recommends a National Farmland Protection Policy as a solution.

5. Michael Bunce, "Agricultural Land as a Real Estate Commodity: Implications for Farmland Preservation in the North American Fringe" (1985), 12 Landscape Planning 177. Bunce provides a cogent argument for a new viewpoint on land that would transcend the conventional notion that prime agricultural land is merely another commodity to be bought and sold in the marketplace. See also L.M. Lavkulich, "Land -- Our Threatened Resource" (1979-80), 11 Journal of Business Administration 265.

6. Royal Commission on the Economic and Development Prospects for Canada, Final Report, 3 Vols. Ottawa: Ministry of Supply and Services. [Hereinafter: Royal Commission]: Vol. 2 at p. 427.

7. Id, pp. 428-9.

7a. For discussion on this point, see Giangrande, Down to Earth, supra note 3 at pp. 25ff.

8. An overview of the dominant ideas about agriculture today is presented in Jack Doyle, Altered Harvest: Agriculture, Genetics and the Fate of the World's Food Supply, (1985). New York: Viking.

8a. Id, pp. 234-78.

8b. Id, pp. 434-45.

9. This survey, which was directed by the Lands Directorate of the federal Department of the Environment, classified land resources into seven categories. According to the categorization, class one land is the best for agricultural purposes, and class seven is of no use for agriculture. The completed results of the survey, published in a massive folio, yields one of the most comprehensive pictures of just how serious the need to promote ALC is in Canada. Most of the information from the study related to agricultural land use change has been

compiled in J.D. McCuaig and E.W. Manning, _Agricultural Land-Use Change in Canada: Process and Consequences_, (1982). Land Use in Canada Series Report No. 21, Lands Directorate, Environment Canada.

10. _Royal Commission, supra_ note 6 at p. 428.

11. C. Leigh Warren and Paul C. Rump, _The Urbanization of Rural Land in Canada, 1966-1971 and 1971-1976_, (1981). Ottawa: Environment Canada, Lands Directorate. Cited in _Royal Commission Id._ at p. 435, note 14.

12. Warren and Rump, _Id._

13. _Royal Commission, supra_ note 6 at p. 428. The Commission is paraphrasing the testimony presented to it by Dr. Manning. This testimony is summarized in "Farmland: The Myth of Plenty" (1984), 1 _Bridges: Explorations in Science, Technology and Social Studies_ 10.

14. _Id_, p. 428.

15. _Id_, p. 429.

16. John Hansen, "Canadian Small Settlements and the Uptake of Agricultural Land, 1966-1976" (1984), 15(1) _Social Indicators Research_ 61.

17. Standing Committee on Agriculture, Fisheries and Forestry, The Senate of Canada, _Soil at Risk: Canada's Eroding Future_, (1984). Ottawa: Ministry of Supply and Services.

18. _Id._, at p. 59.

19. _Id._ One example of this contamination provided in the _Final Report_ of the Macdonald Commission is the build-up of fluoride in soils near Cornwall due to nearby smelters.

20. For a review of the effect of these forces on agriculture, see C.R. Bryant and L.H. Russwurm, "The Impact of Non-farm Development on Agriculture: A Synthesis" (1979), 19 _Plan Canada_ 122. See also, Steiner and Theilacker, _Protecting Farmland, supra_ note 2 at pp. 34-45.

21. K.J. Rhea, _The Prosperous Years: The Economic History of Ontario, 1939-1975_, (1985). Toronto: University of Toronto Press. This trend continues to shape the nature of the Ontario economy according to recent reports in the media: see Orland French, "Services dominate job scene", _The Globe and Mail_, May 15, 1986, p. A7.

22. _Id._, at pp. 40-41.

23. _Id._ at p. 40.

24. Mckie v. K.V.P. Co. Ltd., [1948] 3 D.L.R. 201. A stimulating and critical review of this case is presented in D.P. Emond, "Environmental Law and Policy" (1985) in Consumer Protection, Environmental Law and Corporate Power, Vol. 50 of the Research Studies prepared for the Royal Commission on the Economic Union and Development Prospects for Canada. Toronto: University of Toronto Press.

25. Id, at p. 134. A similar process has been observed in the United States: see F.J. Popper, The Politics of Land Use Reform, (1981). Madison: University of Wisconsin Press; pp. 43-45.

26. Id, at p. 135. This exodus has been described by some American authors in particularly graphic fashion. See, for example, E. Higbee, Farms and Farmers in an Urban Age, (1963). New York: The Twentieth Cenury Fund.

27. Id, at p. 134. The relevant legislation under which this spurt of activity took place was the Planning and Development Act, S.O. 1944, c.16. For a description of the planning powers held under this act and a comparison to the new legislation discussed, infra pp. 15-22 , see D. Hefferon, Land Use Planning: Cases and Materials, (1985-86), 2 Vols. Osgoode Hall Law School, York University, Toronto, Ont.; at pp. 1.1-13.

28. Government of Ontario, Ministry of Treasury, Economics and Intergovernmental Affairs. Design For Development: The Toronto-Centred Region Plan, (1970). Toronto: Queen's Printer. This original policy statement was later modified and the final version was adopted in 1971. The main goal was to promote industrial development within a ninety mile radius of the corner of Queen and Yonge Streets in Toronto. The incentives for this policy were the easily accessible water supply in Lake Ontario and the low cost of servicing new developments in the region. These two features had great appeal to the Conservative government of the day and shaped much of the expansion that has taken place on farmland around Metropolitan Toronto since the policy was endorsed.

For a review of the development of the Toronto-Centred Region Plan and a discussion of the policies that underlay the initiative, see Rhea, Id, pp. 229-233. An economic analysis and critique of the policy is presented in chapter seven of M.W. Frankena and David T. Scheffman, Economic Analysis of Provincial Land Use Policies, (1980). A Research Study prepared for the Ontario Economic Council. Toronto: University of Toronto Press.

29. Rhea, supra note 21 at p. 232.

30. A review of the origins of the models of residential density applied by planners today is presented in William M. Rohe, "Models of Residential Density and Their Impact on Planning: A Historical and Contemporary Analysis" (1982), 7(1) Urbanism Past and Present 15. Rohe traces contemporary ideas

about household density in urbanized areas to the activities of social reformers like Jacob Riis, who "generated much support for city planning by decrying the living conditions in major cities."(at p. 15)

31. E. Howard, Garden Cities of Tomorrow (1925). Cambridge, Massachusetts: The MIT Press. A summary of Howard's ideas and a general introduction to urban planning is Peter Hall, Urban and Regional Planning, 2nd ed., (1982). Harmondsworth: Penguin.

32. F.L. Wright, The Disappearing City, (1932). New York: William, Farquhar and Payson; L. Mumford, Culture of Cities, (1938). New York: Harcourt, Brace and Company.

33. Mumford, Id. at p. 488.

34. For a summary of the planning standards enacted under the Housing Development Act, R.S.O. 1980, c.209., see

35. See discussion infra at pp. 45 - 55. For a general introduction to the subject of housing demand and its relation to other socio-cultural factors, see M. Baldassare, Residential Crowding in Urban America, (1979). Los Angeles: University of California Press.

36. Id, pp. 85-98.

37. D.E. Schmidt et al., "Perceptions of Crowding: Predicting at the Residence, Neighborhood and City Levels" (1979), 11(1) Environment and Behavior 22.

38. See D. Williams and E. Finsler, "Containing Growth Does Save Money" (1978), 44 Planning. 13.

39. R.S.O. 1980 c.379.

40. R.S.O. 1980 c.302.

41. R.S.O. 1980 c.354.

42. R.S.O. 1980 c.368.

43. R.S.O. 1980 c.316.

43a. R. Lang and A. Armour, Municipal Planning and the Natural Environment, Background Report No. 3 prepared for the Planning Act Review Committee, (1977). Toronto: Ministry of Housing.

44. Government of Ontario. Report of the Planning Act Review Committee, April 1977. Toronto: Queen's Printer.

45. Id.

46. Id.

47. Government of Ontario. White Paper on the Planning Act, Background Papers Nos. 1 and 2, May 1979. Toronto: Queen's Printer.

47. Government of Ontario. White Paper on the Planning Act, May 1979. Toronto: Queen's Printer.

48. Government of Ontario. The Planning Act -- A Draft for Public Comment, December 1979. Toronto: Queen's Printer.

49. S.O. 1983, c. 1, as amended by S.O. 1983, c.5 and 82 (revising R.S.O. 1980, c.379). For a general interpretation of the new law in relation to both urban and rural planning, see R. Audet and A. Le Henaff, Land Planning Framework of Canada: An Overview, (1983). Working Paper No. 28, Lands Directorate, Environment Canada.

50. Audet and Henaff, Id, pp. 50-57.

51. The pathbreaking decision which upheld the modern idea of regulation for land use was Village of Euclid v. Ambler Realty Co., (1926) 272 U.S. 365 (U.S.S.C.). This decision was adopted by the Supreme Court of Canada in Re North York By-law 14067, infra note 62.

52. Ottawa v. Boyd Builders, [1965] S.C.R. 408. According to this case the balancing of the municipality's intention against the rights of the landowner is to be assessed through examination of the municipalities actions prior to the attempt by the landowner to exercize his or her rights. If the municipality was acting in good faith and expeditiously, then the court should give them the benefit of the doubt.

53. In contrast to administrative tribunals who are delegated powers and must not fetter these discretionary powers as discussed infra note 171, municipalities are not obligated to exercize discretion in a fair manner and without bias, according to most common law courts. For a recent decision from Britain which held that a County Council could fetter its discretion by making a commitment to undertake a development proposal on community parkland prior to an election, see Steeples v. Derbyshire County Council, [1984] 3 All E.R. 468 (Q.B.D.).

54. S.B. Proudfoot, "The Politics of Approval: Regulating Land Use on the Urban Fringe" (1980), _ Canadian Public Administration _

55. Royal Commission, supra note 6; Vol. 3 at p. __. (see section on final recommendations.)

56. A general introduction to the different undercurrents and ideas about regulation is presented in R.A. Macdonald, "Understanding Regulation by Regulations" (1985) in Regulations, Crown Corporations and Administrative Tribunals, Vol. 48 of the

Research Studies prepared for the Royal Commission on the Economic Union and Development Prospects for Canada. Toronto: University of Toronto Press.

57a. Andrew Roman, "Recent Developments in the "Right" to Participate" (1984) In: N. Bankes and J. Owen Saunders, Public Disposition of Natural Resources: Essays from the the First Banff Conference on Natural Resources Law, Banff, Alberta, April 12-15, 1983. Calgary: Canadian Institute of Resources Law; pp. 155-77.

57. See P. Hogg, Constitutional Law of Canada, 2nd Ed. (1985). Toronto: Carswell. See also P. Russell, "Charterland after one year", (1985), Canadian Public Administration *****

58. See David Fox, Public Participation in the Administrative Process: A Study Paper Prepared for the Law Reform Commission. Administrative Law Series (1979) Ottawa: Law Reform Commission of Canada. At p.138, Fox challenges "the belief that intervenors on the whole merely exploit public forums to irresponsibly express their anger...." He contends instead that present inadequacies cannot be corrected by the dismissal of concerned citizen's efforts:

> Rather, effectiveness and responsibility will increase in proportion to the availability of balanced information sources. Similarly, those who reject participatory techniques on the basis that they may favour special interest groups with experience in the field should consider the fact that an unbalanced forum is corrected not by denying access to all parties, but rather by expanding the number of participants, whether by providing counselling services, procedural handbooks or where possible, simplifying procedure or creating alternative submission techniques such as correspondence records, file or non-adversarial hearings.

59. The Commission report that Cohen is reviewing is Law Reform Commission of Canada, The Legal Status of the Federal Administration, (1985). Working Paper No.40. Ottawa: Law Reform Commission. See David Cohen, "Thinking About the State: Law Reform and the Crown in Canada," Feb. 1986, M.S., 43 pp. at p. 16. Forthcoming, Osgoode Hall Law Journal.

60. [1985] 1 S.C.R. 441.

61. The Ontario Municipal Board Act, R.S.O. 1980, c. 347. The OMB was preceded by the Railway Commission, which existed after the OMB was constituted in 1907, but with reduced powers.

62. The OMB's role in regulating land use planning was confirmed in Re North York By-Law 14067 (1960), 24 D.L.R. (2d) 12. A review of this case and the decision-making patterns of the OMB is found in Marie Corbett, "The Ontario Municipal Board:

Planning and Zoning Cases" (1976), 14 <u>Osgoode Hall Law Journal</u> 93.

63. This classification is derived from Frans F. Slatter, <u>Parliament and Administrative Agencies</u>, (1982). A Study Paper prepared for the the Law Reform Commission of Canada, Administrative Law Series, pp. 8-19.

64. The Board may make general rules regarding its practice and procedure. The Board periodically publishes the Rules of Procedure respecting its operation and jurisdiction. In addition, Ontario Regulation 637, R.R.O. 1980 sets out in section 2 the principle that

> Where any matter is not expressly provided for by these Rules, the Rules of Practice under the <u>Judicature Act</u> shall be followed as they are applicable, as determined by the Board.

Recently, some of the negative perceptions about this arrangement held by lawyers became apparent when the Board drafted a new set of Rules and forwarded them to the Municipal Law Section of the Canadian Bar Association. This section then endeavoured to produce a response under the rubric of a standing committee: see Municipal Law Section, Canadian Bar Association (Ontario), "Interim Report of the Committee on the Rules of the OMB," Feb. 25, 1986. In this report, the Committee has rewritten certain provisions of the Rules to reflect their perceptions of the failings in the operation of the Board. An example of these failings is provided in OMB provisions on cross-examination which the Committee claims amount to "hearing by ambush." See at p. 33 of the Interim Report.

65. Generally the OMB is classified as a quasi-judicial body because it has the power to make rules about its own practices as observed <u>supra</u> note 64. However, their rule-making may be contrasted with a determination-making function. The former generally involves a predetermination of some matter in a way that is binding on cases. Determination-making involves a finding of facts about entitlement to the rights and privileges conferred by social welfare programmes. There has been an attempt recently to inject rule-making into determination in the United States with controversial results. See, discussion <u>infra</u> at pp. 66-70. As Slatter points out in his law reform report, <u>supra</u> note 63, many government departments can generate the advice and develop new procedure required to manage projects and programmes which could duplicate the roles performed by the OMB. Thus, it is the remoteness of administrative tribunals that often has appeal for governments. Probably the most important facet of this remoteness is that tribunals deal with "hot potatoes" and allow the government to give the appearance they are doing something about sensitive matters when they are in fact doing nothing. Another important facet of the insulation role is that it allows government to allocate the benefits of licencing

through a body which appears free of political influence. Where such regulation interferes with vested property rights, the business community is usually happier and public has more faith in the decisions that are made.

For a general discussion on the insulation role of administrative tribunals, see H. N. Janisch, "The Role of Independent Regulatory Agency in Canada" (1978), 27 U.N.B.L.J. 83 at p. 112. See also, J. Evans et al. Adminstrative Law: Cases and Materials, (1984). Toronto: Emond- Montgomery. The latter is the leading textbook at most Canadian law schools and contains excellent commentaries on many of the planning decisions in the Canadian superior courts that are reviewed below as well as comments on adminsitrative tribunals in general terms. For an historical overview on tribunals in Canada, see D.J. Mullan, "Administrative Tribunals: Their Evolution in Canada from 1945 to 1984" (1985) in Regulations, Crown Corporations and Administrative Tribunals, Vol. 48 of the Research Studies prepared for the Royal Commission on the Economic Union and Development Prospects for Canada. Toronto: University of Toronto Press.

67. This argument was made by Prof. D. Hefferon in a class presentation to Land Use Planning, Osgoode Hall Law School, Winter Term 1986. See also Alden Baker, "Municipalities fear interference on planning," The Globe and Mail, Monday, March 28, 1983.

68. On the OMB's capacity to approve official plans under section 12, the leading case is Re Borough of Scarborough and the Minister of Housing for Ontario, et al. (1976), 11 O.R. (2d) 723.

69. Supra note 61.

70. See Corbett, supra note 62 for further discussion on this.

71. Supra note 44.

72. Ontario Government, Report of the Royal Commission on Metropolitan Toronto, (1977). Toronto: Queen's Printer.

73. (1975), 5 O.R. (2d) 401 (Div.Ct.) at p. 411. In this case, a sanitary land fill site was being proposed and the question was whether separate hearings were required before the Environmental Hearing Board (now the Environmental Assessment Board) and the Ontario Municipal Board. The court held that an OMB ruling which held there was no requirement to hear evidence on environmental matters in view of lengthy hearings before the former body was wrong. This problem has now been circumvented by the implementation of the Consolidated Hearings Act, S.O. (1981), c. 20 which amalgamates proceedings of these boards to speed up decision-making. For a review of a decision of the Joint Board established under this Act, see Re County of Oxford Salford Landfill Site (1983), 15 O.M.B.R. 1. The original

decision of the Joint Board, which had been regarded as favourable by environmentalists because it recognized that the proposal was based on inadequate information, was varied by the Ontario Cabinet to allow the County to develop an urgently needed landfill site.

74. D. Estrin and J. Swaigen, Environment on Trial, (1978). Toronto: Canadian Environmental Law Research Foundation.

75. On the matter of onus, there are a range of views that have been offered by the courts which generally affirm there is no onus: see the discussion on this in In Re City of Toronto Restricted Area By-law 258-71 (1973), 2 O.M.B.R. _ at p. 244 the Board took a different view:

> It might be proper at this stage of the decision to reiterate the Board's general philosophy in regard to applications before it for approval of by-laws passed pursuant to s. 35 of The Planning Act, R.S.O. 1970, c.349 which the subject application is. It has long been the Board's practice, in the absence of any opposition that no public hearing be held. In such a case, the Board approves such an application in Chambers. However, where opposition to such an application exists, then the Board requires a public hearing which, inter alia, enquires into the nature of such objections. Therefore, it can be seen that there is no onus on a municipality to 'prove its case as it were'. Where a public hearing is required due to opposition, this general principle remains unchanged. Those who oppose must clearly show that for good reason the Board should withhold its approval. This duty may not be properly called an onus, but there certainly is cast upon objectors the requirement to satisfy this Board that its approval should not be granted for whatever reason they may propose.

Thus, the Board must be satisfied that the applicant council was clearly wrong in enacting the subject by-law, before it will interfere with the decision of duly elected members of Council. Arguably, the onus falls on the aggrieved landowner or citizen's group to prove injury. See Corbett, supra note 62 for discussion.

76. Supra note 74 at pp. 369-70.

77. Id.

78. On this point see the report on the St. James case, O.M.B. File No. 2230. For critical comments on the St. James case, see Estrin and Swaigen at p. 370 and Corbett, supra note 62. All of these authors argue that this case shows that dollar planning is alive and well in Ontario.

79. Some recent OMB decisions which show less interest in conservation-related matters would include, for example, Re South Nation Planning Area Official Plan Amendments; Re Alfred Bog (1983), 16 O.M.B.R. 262. There, Diplock held that privately owned lands could be redesignated to agricultural use even though the local conservation authority had expressed the desire to acquire the land to protect certain species in the bog and the general ecology of the area. See also Hinder v. Metropolitan Toronto Region Conservation Authority (1983), 16 O.M.B.R. 401 where land filling was permitted despite the conservation authority's to preserve the land in an undeveloped state.

80. See Re Toronto - Metro Centre (1974), 2 O.M.B.R. 5 at p.7 where Mr. J.A. Kennedy stated that the "Board 'stands in the shoes' of the Minister." In the result, Kennedy held that the OMB must function "to protect the rights of individuals and minorities but also to see that the provisions of [official] plans follow sound planning principles and are for the benefit of the community."

81. For further disscusion on the idea of an ecology of law, see D. McRobert, "Nibbling Away at the Edges: Towards a Conserver Theory of the Failure of Environmental Law Reform", Unpublished MS., 110 pp. (Available from the author upon request).

82. For a summary of the case law, see Evans et al. supra note 66. See also D. P. Jones and A. de Villars, Principles of Administrative Law, (1985). Toronto: Carswell.

83. [1955] O.R. 83 at p. 91.

84. Id. at p. 96.

85. [1966] 2 O.R. 439 (C.A.). In this case the critical question was whether there was a demand for another regional shopping centre. The OMB held that the consuming public demanded such a centre because they wanted to have access to a range of goods. The Ontario Court of Appeal held that the OMB erred in law when a report was introduced but not brought forward for scrutiny but it would not disturb the decision. The implication of the case is that the OMB has considerable power. It can hear evidence it chooses and rule on matters without following any precedents. Thus, in this case the OMB was effectively determining what the government policy on shopping centre expansion would be because no policy was available at the time. However, as noted in the discussion already, the Board has tended to follow past decisions whenever possible.

86. (1970), 2 O.M.B.R. 1

87. Id, pp. 1-2.

88. Township of Innisfil v. Township of Vespra et al. (1981), 123 D.L.R. (3d) 530 (S.C.C.). [Hereinafter: Innisfil v. Vespra].

89. Re Barrie Annexation (1978), 7 O.M.B.R. 225. The report which launched the action was entitled The Simcoe-Georgian Area Task Force Development Strategy. The County of Simcoe is one of the most popular agricultural and recreational areas in southern Ontario. It is with a touch of irony that I note one of the key factors behind the issue was ALC. The province was trying to discourage growth in the greenbelt around Metropolitan Toronto through promoting the expansion of cities such as Barrie.

90. The legislative authority for an application to alter boundaries is found in the Municipal Act, supra note 40. Section 14 states the OMB has such power but that it must be exercized carefully:

14(2) (a) Upon the application of any municipality authorized by by-law of the council thereof or upon the application of the Minister....the Municipal Board may by order on such terms as it may consider expedient,

　　(b) annex the whole or any part or parts of the municipality to any other municipality or municipalities ....and any such order may amalgamate or annex a greater or smaller area or areas than the area or areas specified in the application....

　　(4) The Municipal Board, before making any order under subsection 2, shall hold a public hearing, after such notice thereof has been given as the Board may direct, for the purpose of inquiring into the merits of the application and of hearing any objections that any person may desire to bring to the attention of the Board.

　　(18) The powers conferred upon the Municipal Board by this section may be exercised at any time or times notwithstanding any other provision in this Act or any other special or general Act and, in the event of any conflict between the provisions of this section and the other provisions of this Act or any other special or general Act, the provisions of this section prevail.

91. Supra note 27.

92. The jurisdiction of the Board and the authority to go to the Court is found in Sections 35 and 95 of the Ontario Municipal Board Act, supra note 61 which state as follows:

35. The Board has exclusive jurisdiction in all cases and in respect of all matters in which jurisdiction is conferred on it by this Act or by any other general or special Act.

95.- (1) Subject to the provisions .... an appeal lies from the Board to the Divisional Court upon a question

91. Supra note 27.

92. The jurisdiction of the Board and the authority to go to the Court is found in Sections 35 and 95 of the Ontario Municipal Board Act, supra note 61 which state as follows:

35. The Board has exclusive jurisdiction in all cases
    and in respect of all matters in which jurisdiction
    is conferred on it by this Act or by any other general
    or special Act.

95.- (1) Subject to the provisions .... an appeal lies
    from the Board to the Divisional Court upon a question
    of jurisdiction or upon any question of law, but such
    appeal does not lie unless leave to......

    (3) On the hearing of any appeal, the court may draw
    all such inferences as are not inconsistent with the
    facts expressly found by the Board and are necessary
    for determining the question of jurisdiction or law,
    as the case may be, and shall certify its opinion to
    the Board and the Board shall make an order in accordance
    with such opinion.

It should be noted that the Court has only the power to certify its opinion back to the Board. In the various Courts, there was much difficulty over this certification and the manner in which it was done.

93. See newspaper article

94. Township of Innisfil et al and the City of Barrie (1978), 17 O.R. (2d) 277.

95. Id, pp. 296.

96. Id.

97. (1971), 3 O.R. 832.

98. Id. cited in supra note 94 aat p. 297.

99. Re Township of Innisfil et al. and the City of Barrie (No. 2) (1978), 7 O.M.B.R. 233. (Div. Ct.)

100. Re Township of Innisfil and Township of Vespra et al. (1979), 23 O.R. (2d) 147. (C.A.).

101. Supra note 85.

102. Supra note 100 at p. 156.

103. Supra note 86.

104. Supra note 50.

105. The provisions of the _Statutory Powers Procedure Act_, S.O. 1980, c. _ which were under consideration are:

3-(1) Subject to subsection 2, this Part applies to proceedings by a tribunal in the exercise of a statutory power of decision conferred by or under an Act of the Legislature, where the tribunal is required by or under such Act or otherwise by law to hold or to afford to the parties to the proceedings an opportunity for a hearing before making a decision.

10. A party to proceedings may at a hearing,

(a) be represented by Counsel or an Agent;

(b) call and examine witnesses and present his arguments and submissions;

(c) conduct cross-examinations of witnesses at a hearing reasonably required for a full and fair disclosure of the facts in relation to which they have given evidence.

15-(1) Subject to subsections 2 and 3, a tribunal may admit as evidence at a hearing, whether or not given or proven under oath or aformation or admissible as evidence in a court,

(a) any oral testimony; and

(b) any document or other thing,

relevant to the subject matter of the proceedings and may act on such evidence, but the tribunal....

Implicit in this legislation is a duty of fairness which the Township of Innisfil felt had been abrogated in the OMB decision to disallow cross-examination as would seem to be provided for under s. 10(c).

106. _Supra_ note 61.

107. _Supra_ note 88 at pp.

108. For a critical overview of this growing concern, see Stephen R. Rodd, "The Crisis of Agricultural Land in the Ontario Countryside" (1976), 16 _Plan Canada_ 160.

109. Government of Ontario. _Food Land Guidelines: A Policy Statement of the Government of Ontario on Planning for Agriculture_, (1978). Toronto: Ministry of Agriculture and Food, Government of Ontario. [Hereinafter: _Guidelines_]. The document was preceded by a discussion paper entitled _A Strategy for Ontario Farmland_ (1976). However, it should be noted that these

provisions do not have the force of law. A Private Member's Bill which would have obliged municipalities to adopt plans in conformity with the Guidelines within two years and frozen non-agricultural land uses on farmland never recieved second reading.

110. Owen J. Furuseth and J.T. Pierce, "A Comparative Analysis of Farmland Preservation Programmes in North America" (1982), 26 The Canadian Geographer 191.

111. Quebec Government. Amenager L'avenir: Les Orientations du Governement en Matiere D'amenagement due Territoire, (1983). (Quebec: Editeur Officiel).

112. Act to Preserve Agricultural Land R.S.Q. 1977, c.P-41-1. This statute permits the government to identify prime agricultural land and create protected zones. The Act then prevents activities which are incompatible with agricultural from being undertaken and controls parcelling of land for subdivisions. Six zones have been established and these cover most of the rural areas of the province.

113. Jane Matthews Glenn, "L'Intervention de L'Etat dans l'Agriculture: Un Apercu Legislatif" (1983), 28 McGill Law Journal 928.

114. R.R. Krueger, "Urbanization of the Niagara Fruit Belt" (1978), 22 The Canadian Geographer 179. For background to the work of Krueger and other prominent researchers such as Gertler, see Orland French, "Bitter Aftertaste of Niagara" The Globe and Mail, Wednesday, _____.

115. Government of Ontario, Niagara Region Local Government Review: Report of the Commission. (1966) Toronto: Department of Municipal Affairs.

116. Regional Municipality of Niagara, Regional Niagara Policy Plan, December 1973. See also the Plan Addenum, 1 October 1974. For a critical overview on the decison, see Rodd, supra at note __.

117. The Minister informed the council by way of a letter in which he stated

> Notwithstanding our commitment to local government, there are certain major land use issues which are considered matters of concern to all of Ontario. These include, for example, ... the fruitland in the Niagara Region and elsehwere, as well as good agricultural land throughout Ontario.

This statement foreshadowed the Food Land Guidelines by more than one year. Cited in Re Niagara 2, infra note 123 at p. 402.

118. Re Niagara Planning Area Official Plan Partial Referral (Niagara Falls, Port Colbourne, Thorold) Urban Area Boundaries (1979), 9 O.M.B.R. 286. [Hereinafter: Re Niagara 1].

119. Klydel Holdings Inc. et al. v. Regional Municipality of Niagara (1979), 10 O.M.B.R. 208.

120. The second petition was Re Klydel Holdings Inc. et al. and the Ontario Municipal Board. Unreported, August 29, 1979. Cited in the second Divisional Court case, Re Klydel Holdings Inc. et al. (1979), 10 O.M.B.R. 203.

121. For the response of Cabinet to the Appeals, see Re Niagara Planning Area Official Plan (1981), 12 O.M.B.R. 296. This statement also contains the new policy on severances discussed infra at pp. _ below.

122. Guidelines, supra note 108.

123. Re Niagara Planning Area Official Plan (1981), 11 O.M.B.R. 353. [Hereinafter: Re Niagara 2].

124. Id.

125. Supra note 108 at pp.

126. Supra note 121 at pp. 297-8.

127. Supra note 122 at pp.

128. John N. Jackson, "The Niagara Fruit Belt: The Ontario Municipal Board Decision of 1981" (1982), 26(2) The Canadian Geographer 172.

129. See French, Supra note 114.

130. H.J. Gayler, "The Problems of Adjusting to Slow Growth in the Niagara Region of Ontario" (1982), 26(2) The Canadian Geographer 165.

131. Id. See also, H.J. Gayler, "Political Attitudes and Urban Expansion in the Niagara Region" (1979), 11 Contact: A Journal of Urban and Environmental Affairs 43.

132. Re Official Plan for the City of Brampton Planning Area (1985), 18 O.M.B.R. 97. [Hereinafter: Re Brampton].

133. Re Mississauga Planning Area Official Plan (A.P.P.E.A.L.) (1981), 13 O.M.B.R. 170. [Hereinafter: Re Mississauga].

134. Supra, note . It was argued in Re Caledon that certain parts of the proposed developments were a logical extension of the northward extension of Brampton's Amendments 26. However, the panel in Re Caledon rejected this because they were not actually considering the latter amendment.

135. The Ministry of Food and Agriculture (MAF) does not have any veto power regarding these decisions but it can express its concerns about proposed changes. Moreover, the _Guidelines_ and the Code of Agricultural Practice require the land owner to consult MAF when there is an intention to sever or develop land. If a perceived or actual conflict emerges, MAF can object to the changes to the official plan, plan amendment, severance, etc. and have a hearing before the OMB: see _Re Ottawa-Carleton Planning Area Official Plan Amendment 25_ (1985), 18 O.M.B.R. 53 at p. 57.

136. _Re Brampton_, supra note 111 at p. 102.

137. _Id_, p. 102.

138. _Id_, p. 117.

139. The _Guidelines_ themselves also reflect the inevitability notion quite explicitly in section 4 C.5(5):

4C.5   Despite the concern with adequate protection
        for agricultural lands, it is recognized that
        all other growth and development cannot and
        should not stop. Historically, many of our
        urban centers have developed in areas of high
        agricultural capability or production, and
        continued growth is necessary. However,
        measures can be taken to minimize the impact
        of this growth on the agricultural areas, or
        to divert it in a direction where agricultural
        capability may be lower.

    5   Where urban growth trends indicate the continued
        absorption of prime food lands, possibilities
        for increasing densities or redirection part of
        the growth to communities situated on lower
        capability food lands should be studied.

Thus, the thrust of the _Guidelines_ in this section is to provide for growth as long as planning considerations are taken into account to minimize ALC and other social costs.

140. Extract from Brampton Official Plan, Cited in _Id_, p. 107.

141. _Id_.

142. _Id_, pp. 119-120.

143. _Supra_ note 109.

144. See John Allemang, "What does the future hold for Brampton?" _The Globe and Mail_, Dec. 14, 1985, pp. G.1-2 at G.2.

145. The statement was broadcast on Radio Noon on Nov. 1985. It was also quoted in Allemang, _Id_.

146. Allemang, Id.

147. Government of Ontario, Foodland Preservation: A Proposed Policy Statement Issued by Government of Ontario for Public Review, February 1986. Toronto: Ministry of Agriculture and Food. [Hereinafter: Foodland Preservation.]

148. Id.

149. See Foodland Guidelines, supra note 108 sections 2.6, 2.7 and 2.8.

150. Supra, note 147 at pp.

151. Id. at pp.

152. Foodland Preservation, supra note _ at p. 6. The specific provision, section 3.1.3, is worded as follows: "To prevent premature commitment of prime agricultural land, the time frame for committing land for future urban development be not more than 10 years."

153. Some recent OMB decisions on severances under the Guidelines are Izusa Investments Inc. v. County of Simcoe L.D. Comm. (1981), 14 O.M.B.R. 121 and Aucillo et al. v. York Regional Land Division Committee (1983), 16 O.M.B.R. 94. In the former, the Board held that an attempt by a farmer to convey severed lots to his children who were 12 and 13 years old at the time and lived 18 miles away from the farm in question was premature under s. 36(4)(b) of the former Planning Act. The OMB rejected a consent to sever "as a means of solving the financial difficulties of the owners of the land" at p. 99.

154. Billiard v. Regional Municipality of Hamilton-Wentworth (1980), 12 O.M.B.R. 123.

155. Id. at p. 125.

156. For a detailed analysis of this problem and its implications for land use control, see C.R. Bryant, L.H. Russwurm and A.G. McLellan, The City's Countryside: Land and its Management in the Rural-Urban Fringe, (1982). New York: Longman. The media have been filled with items about court battles related to nuisance actions against farmers in the past year. See, for example, ***********************

157. Foodland Preservation, supra note _ at pp. 4-5. Under the new provisions for severance, the land parcels that are created must be "sufficiently large to maintain flexibility for future changes" (s. 1.3.1.2.1) in the operation and "viable agricultural units at the time of creation" (s. 1.3.1.2.4) in order to meet the normal requirements.

158. This was an item on Radio Noon, CBC Radio, May 12, 1986.

159. Foodland Preservation, supra note _ at pp. 6-8. Among the criteria listed in the new statement which must be taken into account are the following:

- the amount of existing vacant land
- the potential for infilling existing areas
- projections for land consumption
- land area requirements based on population increases
  assuming "a reasonable density for the municipality
  or planning area under consideration"

The last criteria should be highlighted because it seems to address the problem encountered in Re Brampton head on. However, it is unclear how one would arrive at a "reasonable density and this will no doubt be the subject of future litigation.

In addition to the decisions discussed infra on the question of need, see: Re County of Northumberland Land Fill Site (1982), 15 O.M.B.R. 225; Re Town of Vaughan Planning Area Official Plan Amendment 95 (1980), 13 O.M.B.R. 129; Re Esquesing Planning Area Official Plan Amendment 13 (1983), 16 O.M.B.R. 59; and Re Township of Bosanquet Planning Area Official Plan Amendment 11 (1983), 16 O.M.B.R. 88. None of these decisions offer a clear rule on the issue, however.

For an interesting decision which suggests a pro-conservation stance, see Re Hamilton-Wentworth Planning Area Official Plan Amendment 1 (1980), 13 O.M.B.R. 353. In this decision, the panel held that a zoning amendment sought for a housing complex for senior citizens could not be approved because the land was deemed as agriculturally important. Diplock, vice-chairman of the OMB, stated that the absorption of prime agricultural land "does not make it less important that the municipalities... have regard for boundaries such as have been created in earlier policy statements." However, what really seems to be at work here was politics and power. I would argue the application for amendment was denied on the grounds that the OMB thought the Council's decision demonstrated favouritism towards the applicant.

160. Supra note _ at p.

161. Re Brampton, supra note 132 at p.

162. Environmental impact requirements in Canada were largely imported from the United States where the first statute was enacted in 1969: see National Environmental Policy Act, 1969, 42 U.S.C. 4321-47. For an overview of the development of this legislation and the provincial and federal responses in Canada, see D.P. Emond, Environmental Assessment Law in Canada, (1978). Toronto: Emond-Montgomery.

The relevant legislation in Ontario is the Environmental Assessment Act, R.S.O. 1980 c. . Under the EAA, most government agencies are required to examine a full range of feasible alternatives. For example, the Ministry of Transportation and Communication must consider alternative routes for highways when assessing the impact of their construction on natural environments. It would seem logical to conclude that compliance with the EAA would require municipalities to examine such a range of population growth scenarios.

163. For discussion on this point, see Supra note 2.

164. Supra note 133 at p.24-7.

165. Supra note __ at pp.

166. For a general critique of administrative power and an argument in favour of structuring discretion, see K. Davis' pathbreaking Discretionary Justice, (1969). Baton Rouge: Louisiana State U. Press.

167. Id.

168. Evans et al., supra note 66 present a review of some of the key ideas. A more detailed account of the development of these procedures for structuring discretion in the American courts is M. Verkuil, "The Emerging Concept of Administrative Procedure" (1978), 78 Col. L. Rev. 258. The basic idea is that the agency provides rules which are reviewed by parties affected. Thus, rule-making procedures are undertaken within certain constraints.

169. Re Richmond Hill Planning Area Official Plan (1983), 16 O.M.B.R. 114.

170. Economic Council of Canada, Reforming Regulation (1981). Ottawa: Ministry of Supply and Services; p.130.

171. On the fettering of discretion by the OMB, see Re Hopedale Developments Ltd. and the Town of Oakville, [1965] 1 O.R. 259 (Ont. C.A.). At p. __, McGillivray J.A. held that the OMB " must not fetter its hands and fail, because a guide has been declared, to give the fullest hearing and consideration to the whole of the problem before it...." However, the court did concede that the Board can try to match its decisions with past ones as long as each new case is decided on its merits.

A recent example of an Ontario planning decision where the failure to exercize discretion resulted in an order of mandamus, see Re Multi-Malls Inc. et al. and the Minister of Transportation and Communications et al. (1977), 14 O.R. (2d) 49 (Ont. C.A.). The Charter also has the potential to bring about new developments in this area: see Re Appotive et al. and the City of Ottawa (1983), 16 O.M.B.R. 316 (O.H.C.).

172. Jacques L'Hereux, "Municipalities and the Division of Powers", (1985) in Intergovernmental Relations, Vol. 63 of the Research Studies prepared for the Royal Commission on the

Economic Union and Development Prospects for Canada. Toronto: University of Toronto Press.

173. See Hefferon, supra note _ at p. _ for a discussion on the ability of a municipality to down-zone. Several courts in the U.S. have held that a municipality can down-zone in order to provide for greenspace or control growth. However, the decisions also show that an aggrieved land owner will likely be entitled to compensation. See: Golden v. Planning Board of the Town of Rampo, 285 N.E. (2d) (1972) 291 (N.Y.C.A.); Appeal Dismissed, 93 S.Ct. 440 (U.S.S.C.) and H.F.H. Ltd. v. City of Cerritos (1974), 116 Cal. Rep. 436 (Cal. S. C.).

174. The classic analysis of the implications of the current division of powers on environmental matters for dispute resolution and environmental protection is presented in J.W. MacNeill, Environmental Management (1971). Ottawa: Information Canada. For a more recent assessment and proposals for reform, see D. Gibson, "Constitutional Arrangements for Environmental Protection and Enhancement under a New Canadian Constitution" (1982) in S. M. Beck and I. Bernier (eds.), Canada and the Constitution: the Unfinished Agenda. Montreal: Institute for Public Policy; pp. __.

175. Economic Council of Canada, supra note at p. 127.

176. H. Kitchen and M. L. McMillan, "Local Government and Canadian Federalism" (1985) in Intergovernmental Relations, Vol. 63 of the Research Studies prepared for the Royal Commission on the Economic Union and Development Prospects for Canada. Toronto: University of Toronto Press.

177. Government of Ontario. Financial Impact Analysis: A Handbook for Municipal Planners, (1985). Toronto: Ministry of Municipal Affairs and Housing. Arguably, this desire to make municipalties more self-sufficient is what underlies most of the implicit policies which current development patterns reflect. For example, in the Brampton plan the financial consequences of construction of smaller units for the eventual tax base of the City was a factor. Clearly the municipality wanted to avoid the fact that smaller units require more per caput services than larger ones. It could be argued that the Brampton approach is shortsighted, however. The key disadvantage is that such an approach leads to an unequal spreading the costs and benefits of development throughout the province and tends to produce very rich municipalities in the suburbs who don't have to bear the burden of welfare rolls and other urban phenomena. In this regard, I would contend there is a need to strengthen regional government to promote ALC.

178. See Supra, note _. One of the special issues the Commission addresses is the role of municipalities in the federation. At p. 56 the Commissioners recommend that

The provincial governments should continue to assess possibilities for assuming financial responsibility for requirements greatly exceeding local revenue sources. Commissioners also recommend that the provinces examine ways to designate a specific portion of income or sales-tax revenues for local government financing. Commissioners believe that revenues to local governments should be increasingly unconditional.

179. C.R. Bryant, "Agriculture in an Urbanizing Environment: A Case Study from the Paris Region, 1968-1976" (1981), 25(1) Canadian Geographer 27 at p.28. For more recent work building on Bryant's approach, see E.W. Manning and W.K. Bond, "Land Use Planning and Rural-Urban Conflicts in Ontario: The Role of the Rural Land Owner as a Decision Maker" (1986), MS. 43 pp. (Available from the Author at the Lands Directorate, Environment Canada).

179. Id, p. 29.

180. Id.

181. Id.

182. Id.

183. The Land Speculation Tax Act, S.O. 1974 c. 17. (Repealed after Oct. 24, 1978). A review of the brief history of this legislation is presented in Hefferon, supra note _ at p. 11.1.25.

184. see D. Hefferon, The British Land Commision and the Betterment Levy (1970), Unpublished MS., Reproduced in part in supra note __ at pp. 11.1.13 - 24; at p. 11.1.13.

185. Rebecca Conard, "Green Gold: 1950s Greenbelt Planning in Santa Clara County, California" (1985), 9(1) Environmental Review 5.

186. William Smith, "The 'Vortex Model' and the Changing Agricultural Landscape of Quebec" (1984) 28(4) The Canadian Geographer 358.

187. Ibid at p. 371.

188. For an outline of agricultural practices in a conserver society, see B. Warkentin, "Agriculture, Food and Renewable Resources in a Conserver Society" (1976) in K. Valakakis et al. (eds.) The Conserver Society Project, Vol. 2. University of Montreal/McGill University: GAMMA.

For a leading case on the interpretation of this statute, see _Re Central Ontario Coalition Concerning Hydro Transmission Systems et al._ (1985), 27 M.P.L.R. 165 (Ont. Div. Ct.).

122a.

123.

124. _Foodland Preservation_, _supra_ note _ at pp. 4-5

126. _Supra_ note

176. See _White Paper_, _supra_ at note _. In Chapter Six at sections 6.7 - 6.8, the province agrees with the general approach of the Comay Report on the need for regional planning. One recommendation made in this study was that upper-tier plans prepared would be dominant under the new legislation. It appears that this idea is reflected in provisions which require a lower tier municipal plan to conform with that of an upper tier plan. See section __.

Table 1 - Volume of Agricultural Production in Ontario
from 1941 - 1975 (1961 = 100)

Index Numbers of Physical Volume of Agricultural Production,
Ontario 1941–75 (1961 = 100)

Year	Number	Year	Number
1941	65.6	1959	90.6
1942	77.1	1960	93.5
1943	58.4	1961	100
1944	71.8	1962	105.1
1945	64.4	1963	106.4
1946	70.4	1964	108.9
1947	66.6	1965	108.6
1948	70.3	1966	118.0
1949	73.5	1967	114.6
1950	73.0	1968	118.5
1951	75.8	1969	117.7
1952	77.5	1970	124.6
1953	77.5	1971	127.9
1954	77.6	1972	125.3
1955	78.9	1973	122.4
1956	80.0	1974	129.5
1957	84.7	1975	135.3
1958	93.2		

SOURCE: Ontario, Ministry of Agriculture and Food, *Agricultural Statistics for Ontario 1941–1978* (Toronto, 1979), table 1:4, 6

From: Rhea, *The Prosperous Years: An Economic History of Ontario 1939 - 1975.* (1985)

Table 9

Legislation concerning Protection of Natural and Built Environment in Ontario

Province	Act, Regulation	Type of Control	Those Affected	Control Mechanisms
Ontario	Niagara Escarpment Planning and Development Act RSO 1980 c. 316	Special designation of area	Residents of designated area	Plan prepared by Niagara Escarpment Commission should contain policies on private and public land planning. The Minister of Treasury and Economics regulates development in the region and issues development permits.
	Parkway Belt Planning and Development Act RSO 1980 c. 368	Designation of green belt	Residents of designated area	This green belt serves to divide and delineate urban and rural regions.
	Environmental Protection Act RSO 1980 c. 141	Analysis criteria used to control pollution and noise level and establish standards for sanitary waste fills and waste treatment plants	Developers and development agencies	Development plans must contain and respect criteria specified in the Act. Development permits are required.
	Ontario Planning and Development Act RSO 1980 c. 354	Development plan	Individuals resident in development area	Plan must contain policies concerning population, land use, land and water management, control of environmental pollution, location and development of public utilities. Regulations are enforced.

From: R. Audet and A. Le Henaff, Land Planning Framework in Canada: An Overview (1983)

Table 3.

Page 107

Table 3 - Legislation Related to Agricultural Land Conservation in Canada From: R. Audet and A. Le Henaff. Land Planning Framework in Canada: An Overview (1983).

Province	Act, Regulation	Type of Control	Those Affected	Control Mechanisms
Alberta	Planning Act RSA 1980 c. P-9	Zoning and subdivision	Land owner, Municipalities	Criteria and standards for development/re-development
British Columbia	Agricultural Land Commission Act	Agricultural zoning by the province	Land owner, Municipalities	Municipalities must designate agricultural land in their development and community plans.
Manitoba	Planning Act SM 1975 c. 29	Development plan	Municipalities	Plan must contain proposals for management as well as for preservation of agricultural land and related activities
Newfoundland	Development Areas (Land) Act	Agricultural zoning by the province	Land owner, Municipalities	Agricultural reserves are identified in municipal zoning plan in the Avalon Peninsula.
Nova Scotia	Planning Act SNS 1969 c. 16	Development plan	Land owner, Municipalities	Urban expansion is limited, and development on CLI land classes 2 and 3 is not permitted.
Ontario	Foodland Guidelines	Rural zoning	Municipalities	Usable zones may be designated by municipalities/regions. Checks are made on basis of municipal plan.
Québec	An Act to Preserve Agricultural Land	Agricultural zoning by the province	Land owner, Municipalities, Municipalities	Local municipalities and MRC must designate agricultural land in their plans.

Figure 1 - Maps Showing Percent Change in Farmland Area in Eastern and Western Canada.

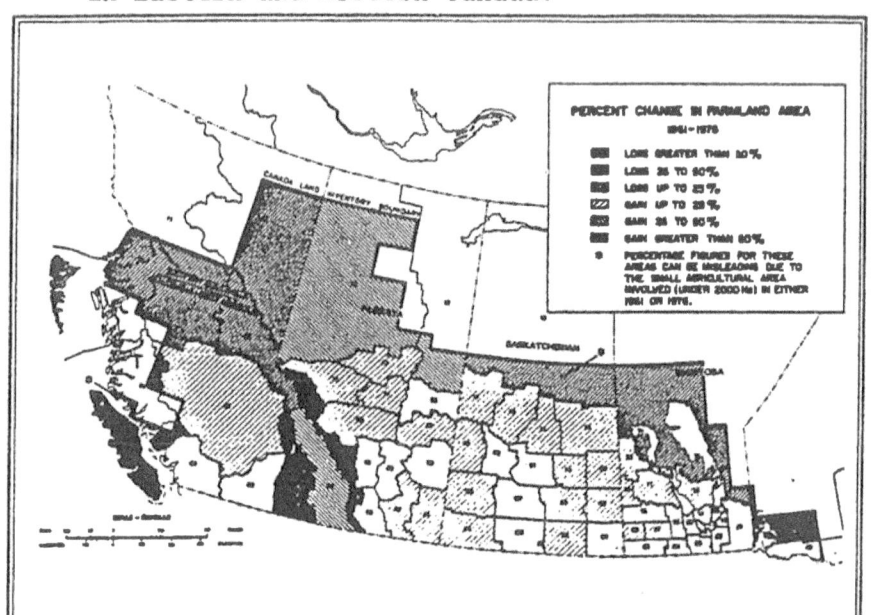

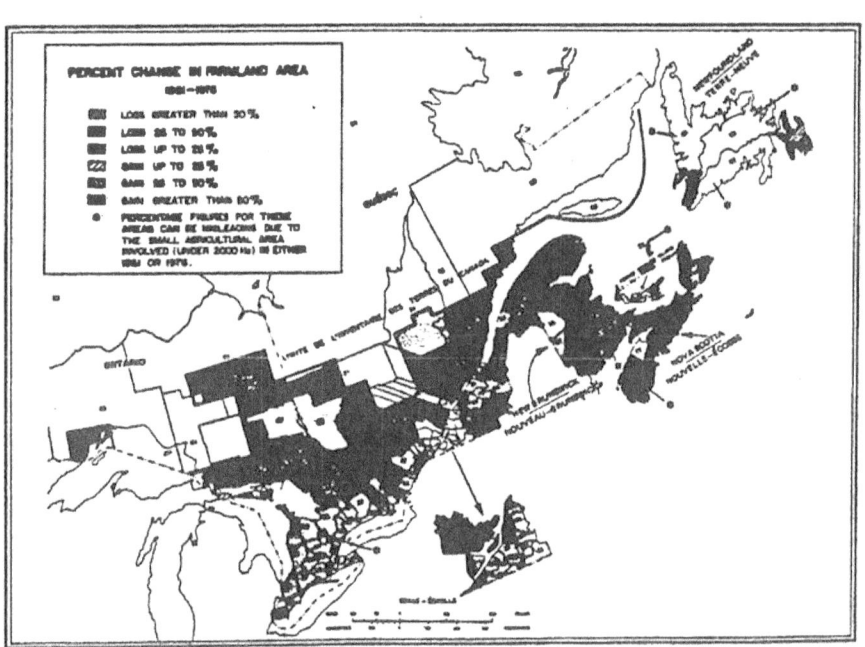

From: J.D. McCuaig and E.W. Manning, Agricultural Land Use in Canada: Process and Consequences, (1982).

Figure 2 - Approval Procedure for An Official Plan in Ontario

The council of a municipality may approve for the preparation of an official plan (with the approval of the Minister)

One public meeting is required during the preparation of the plan

The municipal council may adopt the plan as a by-law and submit it to the Minister for his approval

Minister approves the official plan or parts of the plan or can make modifications

.....Any requests for amendments to the official plan are presented to the Minister who can then refer the matter to the OMB if it is not of provincial interest.

From: R. Audet and A. Le Henaff, Land Planning Framework in Canada: An Overview (1983).

Figure 3 - Farmland Protection Mechanisms in Canada and the United States.

	Differential Tax Assessment	Circuit Breaker Taxation	Centralized Land Use Policies	Agricultural Land Banking	Transfer of Development Rights	Exclusive Agricultural Zoning	Agricultural Districting	Executive Powers Actions	Waiver of Urban Infra-structural Assessment
CANADA									
ALBERTA	●		●						●
BRITISH COLUMBIA	●		●	●		●			●
MANITOBA			●						
NEW BRUNSWICK	●		●						●
NEWFOUNDLAND	●		●			●			●
NOVA SCOTIA	●		●						
ONTARIO	●		●						
PRINCE EDWARD I.	●		●	●			●		●
QUEBEC	●		●	●		●			●
SASKATCHEWAN	●		●	●					
UNITED STATES									
ALABAMA	●								
ALASKA	●				●				
ARIZONA	●								
ARKANSAS	●								
CALIFORNIA	●		●						
COLORADO	●								
CONNECTICUT	●				●				
DELAWARE	●								
FLORIDA	●								
GEORGIA									
HAWAII	●		●	●		●			●
IDAHO	●								
ILLINOIS	●							●	
INDIANA	●								
IOWA	●								
KANSAS	●								
KENTUCKY	●								
LOUISIANA	●								
MAINE	●								
MARYLAND	●				●		●		●
MASSACHUSETTS	●			●	●				
MICHIGAN		●							
MINNESOTA	●						●		●
MISSISSIPPI									
MISSOURI	●								
MONTANA	●								
NEBRASKA	●								
NEVADA	●								
NEW HAMPSHIRE	●				●				
NEW JERSEY	●								
NEW MEXICO	●								
NEW YORK	●						●		
NORTH CAROLINA	●								
NORTH DAKOTA	●								
OHIO	●								
OKLAHOMA	●								
OREGON	●	●				●			●
PENNSYLVANIA	●		●						
RHODE ISLAND	●								
SOUTH CAROLINA	●								
SOUTH DAKOTA	●								
TENNESSEE	●		●						
TEXAS	●								
UTAH	●								
VERMONT	●								
VIRGINIA	●						●		●
WASHINGTON	●		●						
WEST VIRGINIA	●								
WISCONSIN		●	●			●			●
WYOMING	●								

From: O.J. Furuseth and J.T. Pierce, "Farmland Preservation Programmes in North America" (1982).

Figure 4 — Map Showing Agricultural Land in Brampton
which is the subject of the current
Cabinet Appeal.

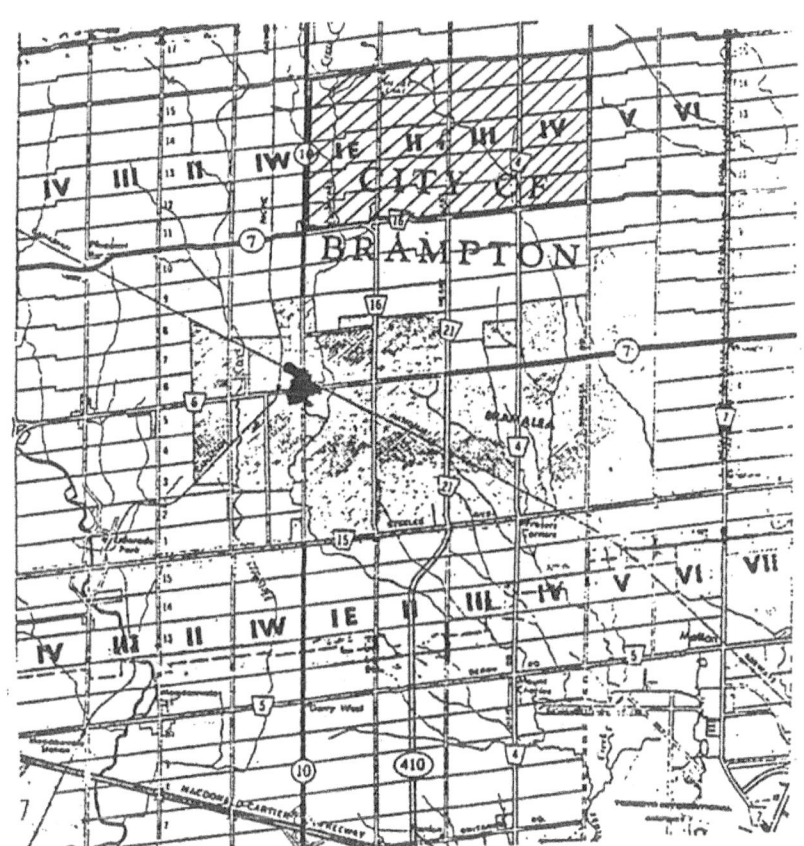

Figure 5 - Two Maps Showing the Impact of the OMB and Cabinet
Decisions on Urban Boundaries in the Niagara Region.

From: Gayler (1982).

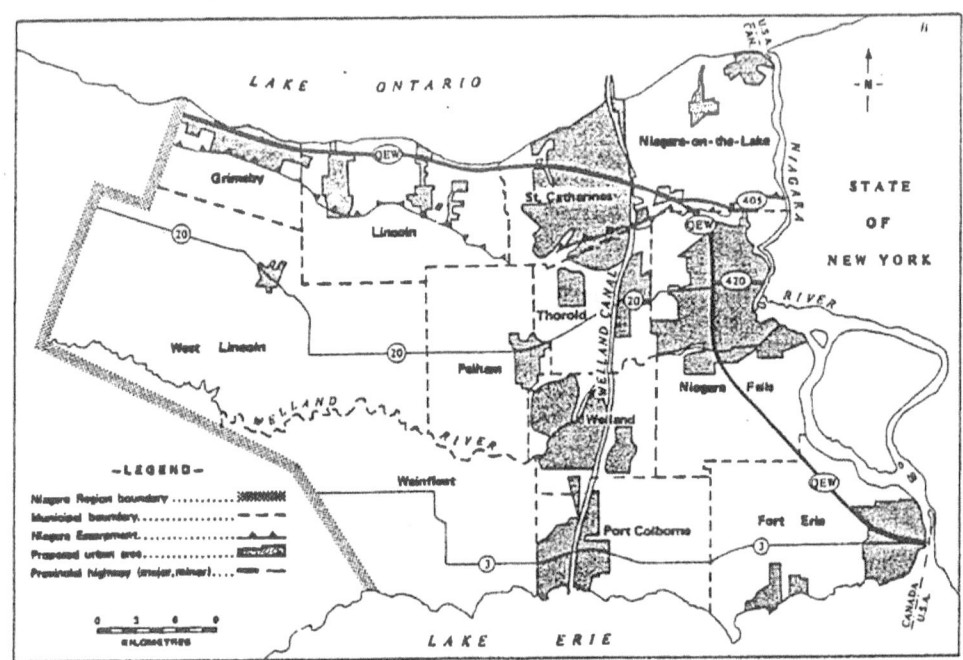

5 (a) Regional Niagara policy plan- proposed urban
area boundaries, 1974.

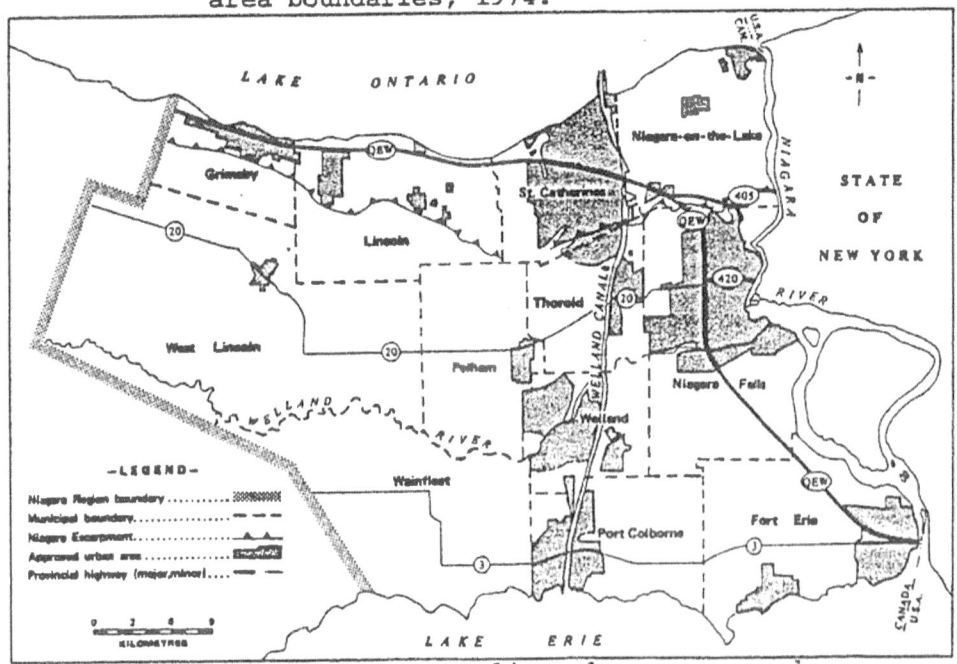

5 (b) Regional Niagara policy plan - approved
urban area boundaries, 1981.

Figure 6 - Conceptual Framework Concerning Forces at Work
         in Land Use Change in the Rural-Urban Fringe.

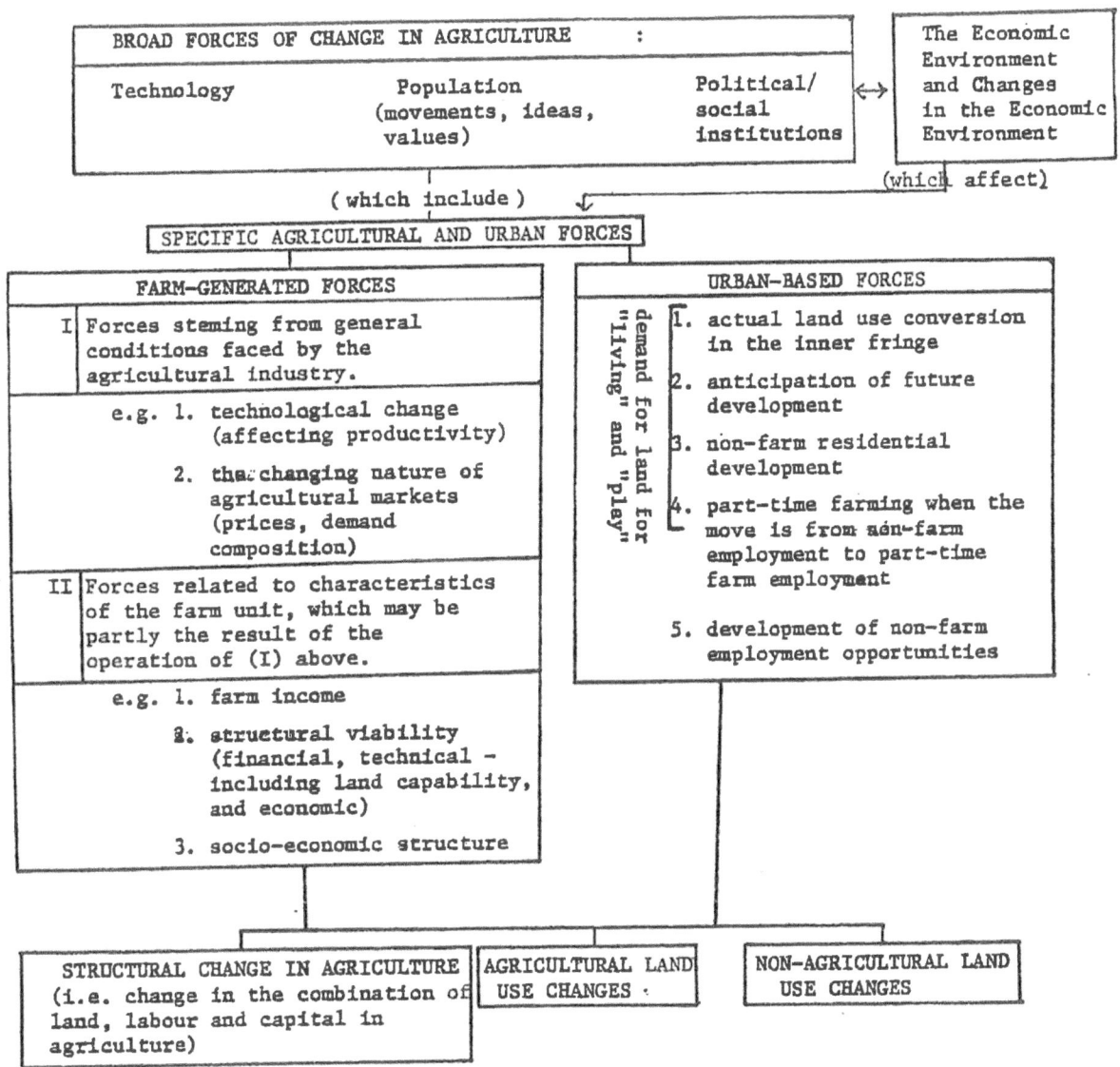

From: C.R. Bryant, Farm-Generated Determinants of Land Use
      Changes in the Rural-Urban Fringe in Canada, 1961-1975
      (1976).

a. The Food-Supply System: Its Levels

b. The Structure of the Levels in Quebec

Consumers

Retailers

Wholesalers

Processors

Farmers

Note:
Price formation occurs
in classical sense between
the levels: a classic supply
and demand curve. Compe-
tition (in classical sense)
occurs among the actors
at one particular level.

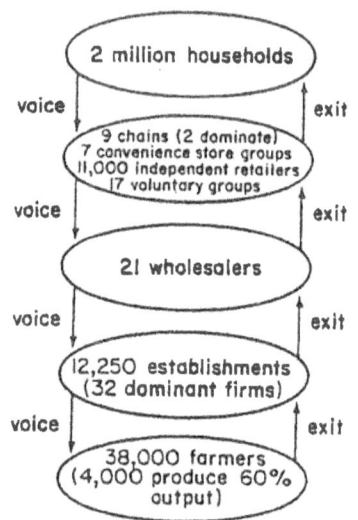

2 million households

voice — exit

9 chains (2 dominate)
7 convenience store groups
11,000 independent retailers
17 voluntary groups

voice — exit

21 wholesalers

voice — exit

12,250 establishments
(32 dominant firms)

voice — exit

38,000 farmers
(4,000 produce 60%
output)

c. The Food-Supply System Nests in a
Superstructure of Government (state)
Legislation and Controls

Note:
The ties between levels
are more important than
within a level, so far as
transformation of the
system is concerned

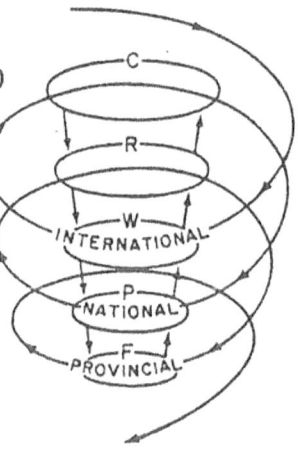

Figure 7 — The Food Supply System: its levels
and Structure.

From: Smith (1982)